Come, Let Us Worship

Come, Let Us Worship

A Concerned Call to Appraisal

by
James R. Spruce

Beacon Hill Press of Kansas City
Kansas City, Missouri

ISBN: 083-411-0288

Printed in the United States of America

Cover Art: Royce Ratcliff

10   9   8   7   6   5   4   3   2   1

To
my parents,
Fletcher and Irene Spruce,
who expressed holy joy in such
wonderfully quiet ways.

Contents

Foreword

Worship is the highest act of which a creature of God is capable. "The chief end of man is to glorify God and enjoy Him forever." In worship we experience the summum bonum of our existence, the ultimate fulfillment and bliss of our creaturehood.

By the same token, the highest act of the church is corporate worship. As the people of God we gather together to ascribe to Him "worthship," to give Him the worth, the honor, the glory which are His due as God, our Creator and Redeemer. As those who have been washed in the blood of Jesus we sing with the heavenly beings, "Worthy is the Lamb that was slain to receive power, and riches, and wisdom, and strength, and honour, and glory, and blessing" (Rev. 5:12).

In the life of the church no other activity can be compared with worship. Worship is the vital spark of heavenly flame that inspires, promotes, refines, and sustains the life of the soul. It is the entrance into the throne room of heaven. To worship is to say, "I saw also the Lord . . . high and lifted up" (Isa. 6:1). It is to be bathed in the Shekinah of God.

William Temple has given a comprehensive, now classic, definition: "Worship is the quickening of the conscience by the holiness of God; it is the nourishment of our mind by the truth of God; it is the purifying of our imagination by the beauty of God; it is the opening of our heart to the love of God; it is the surrender of our will to the purpose of God—and all of this gathered up in adoration, the most selfless emotion of which human nature is capable and therefore the chief remedy for that self-centeredness which is our original sin."

When all has been said, the church's only excuse for existence is to provide a place for worship, a place where mortals can respond with all their heart and soul and mind to the mystery, the majesty, and the mercy of God. Every activity in which the church is engaged must lead to this one grand end, the worship of God.

It was such a vision of the church as a worshiping community which prompted Dr. Phineas F. Bresee's repeated plea to early Nazarenes, "Keep the glory down!" It is a reminder we desperately need today. John R. Stott has written: "We evangelicals do not know much about worship. Evangelism is our specialty, not worship. We have little sense of the greatness of Almighty God. . . . Our worship services are often ill-prepared, slovenly, mechanical, perfunctory, and dull. . . . Much of our public worship is ritual without reality, form without power, religion without God."

A deep concern that we examine our public worship prompted Pastor James R. Spruce to write this book. He writes as a Nazarene elder, an acknowledged free-church Protestant with one final bias—"To oppose worshiping the Almighty by offering Him our casual, unplanned confusion."

This is not a volume to be read casually. Designed primarily for pastors, it also speaks cogently to anyone concerned with the renewal of Nazarene worship. Like Robert E. Webber, Spruce knows that "worship is a verb." It is something that people of God must *do*. These pages are offered as a guide to pastors and people who are concerned to make the worship of God what it should truly be. Even those who do not choose to follow the activities or utilize the tools offered in chapter 5 will find information, inspiration, and practical guidance here in refining the public worship of God.

—WILLIAM M. GREATHOUSE
General Superintendent

Preface

This book is a modest attempt to encourage the assessment of congregational worship by pastor and people within the local Church of the Nazarene. It is not intended to set forth a theology of worship, nor to be a scholarly review of this field. My conviction is that our worship has been given less priority than it deserves, and that both pastor and laity may profit from responsible mutual worship appraisal done in a spirit of compassionate candor. The intent is not to suggest change in worship style, nor to establish a perfect worship model. The goal is to enable worship leader and worshiper to assess their feelings, perceptions, misperceptions, and expectations of worship.

I feel that it is especially important for the Nazarene reader to see the history of Nazarene worship in light of the history of Christian liturgy. This needs to be done in order to assess worship against the backdrop of encroaching social and moral value changes that are affecting us today. Because of this, the pastor must earn the right to call his people to assessment. And the congregation, in fulfillment of their role as true New Testament "ministers," must respond in faithfulness to appraise their *own* worship life.

The reader should know that I write with personal and professional bias. First, I believe that the energy, resources, and commitments of the laity regarding worship renewal are dormant within many of the more theologically conservative churches. Second, I write as a pastoring Nazarene elder which means that I am not a high-church liturgist. As a member of free-church Protestantism, I value deeply my own theological and doctrinal position that has room aplenty for human expressions of praise, testimony, and joy in the Lord during worship services.

Third, I write with profound respect for worship traditions different from my own. Cultural disparity, personality differences, worship style preferences, differing heritages, simple likes and dislikes, biblical interpretation, and the advancement from a rural to a high-tech society all contribute to a variety of worship practices and customs. Who knows but that God appreciates the varying ways His children worship Him? I have tried not to judge the ways of the worshiper.

But I do write with one final bias, which is that I oppose worshiping the Almighty by offering Him our casual, unplanned confusion. Certainly the fact that God honors His people and is patient with us does not mean that we have the freedom to enter into His presence irreverently, haphazardly, or unconcernedly ignorant of the blessings that may result from intentional worship assessment.

My debt to those laypersons in my pastorates who have been so courageous as to take seriously their ministry of worship assessment is beyond measure. My thanks is extended to Dr. William Greathouse, general superintendent of the Church of the Nazarene, for his valuable criticism, and to Nazarene elder Mark Goodwin for his suggestions. Both Dr. Dwight Uphaus and Dr. Roger Hahn of Bethany Nazarene College, Bethany, Okla., have given excellent insight. My deepest appreciation is offered to my best friend and critic, my wife, Karen.

But my reward will be in the reader who, in searching for ways to assess his worship, gets lost—lost in wonder, love, and praise.

Acknowledgments

Grateful acknowledgment is made to the following publishers and other copyright holders for permission to use the copyrighted selections in this book:

Christian Ministry for a selection from "If I Were to Build Again," by Martin E. Marty, copyright 1978, by *Christian Ministry*.

Christianity Today for a selection from "Moneychangers in the Church: Making the Sounds of Music," by Richard D. Dinwiddie, copyright 1981, by *Christianity Today*. For a selection from "Church Management: The Architecture of Ministry," by Norman Shawchuck, copyright 1979 by *Christianity Today*. For a selection from "Transcendence: Now a Secular Quest," by John R. W. Stott, copyright 1979 by *Christianity Today*.

Carl S. Dudley for permission to adapt the "affectional" and "directional" Christian concept for use in a survey tool, taken from Affectional and Directional Orientations to Faith, The Alban Institute, Mount St. Alban, Washington, D.C.

Leadership for a selection from "Worship: Preparing Yourself and Your Congregation," by Terry C. Muck, ed., copyright 1981 by *Leadership*. For a selection from "Worship as Performance," by Ben Patterson, copyright 1981, by *Leadership*.

New English Bible (NEB), © The Delegates of the Oxford University Press and The Syndics of the Cambridge University Press, 1961, 1970.

The Holy Bible, New International Version (NIV), copyright © 1973, 1978, 1984 by the International Bible Society.

Preacher's Magazine for a selection from "Worship as the Recognition of the Holy," by William M. Greathouse, copyright 1980, by *Preacher's Magazine*. For a selection from "Music and the Worship of God," by Donald Hustad, copyright 1980, by *Preacher's Magazine*. For a selection from "A Little Old Lady's Question," by Neil B. Wiseman, copyright 1980, by *Preacher's Magazine*. For a selection from "Worship—More than a Spectator Sport," by Neil B. Wiseman, copyright 1980, by *Preacher's Magazine*.

1

Problem

The Risk
of Giving Sanctuary
to Worship

"Hide It Under a Bushel? No!"

The scenes are nearly sacred to my memory. I remember kneeling next to my praying preacher-father around the old altar rail in the Quindaro Church of the Nazarene.* I can hear his quiet groans in the spirit even yet. People knelt everywhere in various positions; I remember, for I used to steal a glance now and then.

I recall with warmhearted joy the evangelistic services which often lasted two weeks or more. These revivals were abbreviated versions of the "protracted meetings," and the evangelist usually stayed at our parsonage. Services were marked with jubilant singing and seemingly marathon preaching. I remember nights when we hung kerosene lanterns around the sanctuary walls, not for light, but for special effect to highlight the lingering memory of pioneer

---

*Now the Victory Hills Church of the Nazarene, Kansas City, Kans.

15

services. Men wore bib overalls and women wore floor-length print dresses to remind one another of the old days. I recall lengthy testimonies, shouts of joy and victory, and altar services that lasted upwards of an hour after the hour-long service. I remember when nearly everybody prayed aloud at one time.

My young life was enriched by the flavor of camp meeting services at a place called Scottsville Holiness Camp near Marshall, Tex. Every summer for nine years we traveled to this rugged campsite, deep in the piney woods of east Texas. There sawdust covered the floor and cobwebs covered the rafters. The pews were hard to sit on, and the air dripped with the muggy heat of many a summer night. June bugs swarmed around the light bulbs that swung from wooden beams. My grandfather, my father, and I all knelt at different times across the years at the altar rail of this holiness-heritage landmark.

Again the singing and preaching were typically warm-hearted, contagious, sometimes nearly bordering on the boisterous. And we loved it! It seemed that evangelism always prevailed as the dominant theme. Soon the mood of the hour, most always that of genuine conviction, settled in. Once the altar call was given, people swarmed to the place of prayer—the mourner's bench, marking the end of a sawdust trail.

As I grew older and Dad assumed another pastorate, I took note of the fact that services were marked with the stately quality of a magnificent pipe organ. I was a midteen before it dawned upon me that we were following a printed order of worship in the Sunday morning bulletin. There seemed to be a rhythm to worship.

But there was always room in our worship setting—printed agenda or not—for the "interruption" of God! At about 15 I remember clearly a man who came to the altar as the offering was being received. Others followed. The service lasted until well after lunch with no singing or preaching. I remember because I was getting hungry. And I was a seeker in that service, too. Worship was always marked, in my memory, by the absence of formality and the presence of "freedom in the Spirit" as we called (and call) it.

Once in college and again in seminary I recall services that began at the appointed morning worship hour and lasted until late afternoon. Folks usually wanted to "get out before noon," but those same people would stay and pray or sing or stand around and visit long past closing time on many occasions.

These are a few of my personal early memories of public Christian worship among Nazarenes. They are dear to my heart and clear in my mind. I would not change them; indeed, I encourage them.

I have learned that it is appropriate to harbor the long-silent but treasured memories of worship. So, for most of my adult life, I have given sanctuary or protective refuge to my feelings about Christian worship. I have resisted self-initiated attempts to examine and change parts of church life with which I felt comfortable. And I have been most comfortable with church worship.

But being comfortable with my memories is not necessarily the same as being accountable with my role as a worshiper and worship leader. While I honor my memories of church worship, I do not worship in the same atmosphere and in the same way I did 30 years ago. Few aspects of church life remain static and at the same time healthy. Nazarenes still may enjoy the spirit of the early pioneers who founded their denomination, but some of our customs and practices in worship are different.

The unique position Nazarenes are in today, more than 75 years since the 1908 organization at Pilot Point, Tex., is one of honest appraisal and assessment. Both historical and theological roots which stem from our Wesleyan-Arminian heritage are distinct because we have not divorced ourselves from our history. But neither have we refused to face the demands of this present age. And one of the rising challenges before us now is to determine if we will be faithful in the assessment of a relatively unassessed area of congregational life—public worship. Thus a factor that is having influence upon us today is the near vacuum within which our people have appraised congregational worship, at least historically and biblically.

This is certainly not to say that worship among Nazarenes is undeveloped, but rather to suggest that we have simply emphasized other aspects such as discipling, church growth, evangelism, and so on, rather than any phase of congregational worship. Since we are not of a more "formal" tradition, our worship expressions are embedded in a religion that is "better felt than telt." And rightly so, for Nazarenes! For we came into being to express a heartfelt religion that would enable us to evangelize lost sinners and teach them how to live a holy life in a sinful world.

And in the grand spirit of such a direction, we have had phenomenal growth. We enjoy diverse ministries and spiritual gift development within the local church level. Denominationally, we extend into some 75 world areas. We prosper under the financial commitment of people who are largely sacrificial and come from all walks of life. And we have hardly paused long enough to catch our breath. Nor must we! But none of this means we should be painfully awkward about attempts to assess ourselves—even in perhaps the most unassessed area of all, congregational worship.

An unfortunate consequence is that since worship assessment among Nazarenes has been so often overshadowed by other dimensions of church life, few of us are in position to appraise worship, nor to deal faithfully with misperceptions that develop within the local church. In a state approaching near worship passivity, most of us take neither the time nor energy to examine attitudes, plans, and evaluations for the future. Worship has just not received all that much attention from us.

A larger framework for this state of affairs is provided by Nazarene elder Neil B. Wiseman: "True worship is the missing factor in many of our churches. We work. We organize. We preach. We have nice people. We have beautiful sanctuaries. And we have good equipment. But frequently we do not have the ability to worship."[1] Church growth specialist C. Peter Wagner of Fuller Theological Seminary quotes Raymond Ortlund: " 'Worship is lofty business—but friend, we do it so poorly.' "[2] Wiseman and Ortlund, in essence, have summed up the problem: While doing the work of God, we have somehow neglected the worship of God, and the work of worship.

What has happened, then, is that we have unwittingly given sanctuary to worship. We have sheltered and protected our perceptions—and our misperceptions—about this most sacred of Christian events. We have not been ready to separate our feelings about past experiences and memories from current need and mission. The risk we face is not only that of losing our pioneer spirit of evangelistic warmheartedness but also that of sacrificing worship mission for worship sentiment.

Because worship is such a sacred privilege and responsibility, we approach it cautiously and reverently, fearing lest we tamper and meddle with the very activity of God among His people. The consequence may be that by unintended default we allow worship to become the untouchable "sacred cow," while all else is subjected to our most careful study. Such a mentality is unwarranted, in my opinion, if worship is our most sacred joy within the church.

Books, articles, and seminars abound to aid our study of church growth methods, evangelism techniques, population shifts, and census projections. But little, if anything, is suggested about assessing or understanding public worship. Pastors and denominational leaders have rightly assumed that worship is within the pastor's care. But we have wrongly assumed that worship is the exclusive domain of the pastor, and that the laity have no responsible role in worship assessment. Moreover, we have wrongly assumed that everyone holds accurate worship perceptions in the first place.

The focus of this study, then, is upon the vitalization of worship by gathering our sense of history and facing unique worship tensions in order to enable the laity to deal faithfully with their assessments and perceptions. Paul W. Hoon, noted theologian and liturgist, addresses the dilemma faced when considering assessment:

> The fact is that ignorance of the meaning of worship is so widespread among the laity of free-church Protestantism as to be virtually disabling. A number of influences account for this ignorance . . . : the absence of any unifying liturgical ethos in our religiously pluralistic culture; the secularization of people's perceptions; the anti-historical bias which Sidney Mead has called "historylessness;" the subjectivism and voluntarism with which the typical layman decides what is important to him.[3]

In order for churches to be faithful it will be necessary for them to examine both their misperceptions and their own sense of history. But for this to happen, we will need to ask, "What *is* supposed to happen when the people of God meet for worship?" Thus it is necessary to examine the secularization of perceptions, the sense of history (or lack of it), and the privately held feelings which we all have that may lead to confusion in the theology, planning, and purpose of worship.

Admittedly, this is risky business. We are not often prepared to think both compassionately and critically together. The assessment of worship is typically the duty of the pastor, and it is my conviction that in the main, it is passively ignored by the laity. But the laity are not to be faulted. Worship leaders must encourage and assist laypersons in identifying worship interests and commitments so that they may face what they do with integrity.

We have reasoned that worship is the pastor's job since he organizes, leads, and somehow ministers to the congregation through the service. After all, in places where the biblical concept of lay ministry is not encouraged, people may see the pastor as *the* minister. If the laity do not see themselves as "ministers" (in the New Testament sense of the term), confusion related to responsible role development occurs.

Apathy, then, results when the laity have no opportunity for self-expression, or where no forum for assessment and dialogue between pastor and laity exists. As McCormick Theological Seminary Prof. Robert Worley warns,

> Few congregations have participated in congregational processes for understanding their worship life and transforming that life to make it . . . vital and central. . . . It remains an activity primarily related to the pastor's performance, not the congregation's participation in worshiping God.[4]

Thus it is with no trouble at all that we give undue sanctuary to congregational worship. Trying to evaluate the work of God among His people in such a subjective area as worship has not been the thing to do. After all, who *should* tell if we worship well? Is it really necessary to ask such a question? Is not God pleased with whatever worship we offer Him? And who should ever have the right to imply that worship is *not* well? These questions do have the ring of sincerity because they are being asked by honest persons.

And yet folks who take their worship seriously would admit that, of all church activities, worship is worthy of our best attention. For who among us has not wondered, at least occasionally, Is what we are doing on Sunday morning evidence of the *best* we may offer our Lord? The rationale for such a question—and for such a book as this—is set forth by a Catholic theologian named Hans Küng: "A truthful church does not give man any cheap recipes for his private life . . . but it gives man ground under his feet, letting him know his whence and whither, his why and to what purpose."[5] It is my belief that providing opportunity for the laity to evaluate worship with their pastor is the beginning in offering sound footing for the revitalization of this feature of the church's life.

The intention here is not to encourage mere academic criticism so that worship life might be assessed in some ivory tower lab. Getting lost in the paralysis of analysis is a jungle from which few return the wiser. The hope is that our public expressions of a religion that has been so meaningful and joyous for us will not become diluted because we honor sentiment more than mission. While the line between criticism and solution may be thin, it is certainly worthy of our Christian response.

The next chapter will provide an overview of Christian worship, so that we may see how the Church of the Nazarene and its worship practice fits in.

2

Perspective

Nazarene Worship
in Historical Perspective

"O God, Our Help in Ages Past"

Nazarene worship does not stand apart from history. In this chapter we will give attention to Old and New Testament worship practices, plus the influence of several major Reformers during the rise of Protestantism in the period of the Reformation. Then we will consider contributions of the Wesleys in England in the 1700s and 1800s, with the spread of Methodism to the American frontier. This will offer a sense of history and connection with camp meeting life and revivalism as the Church of the Nazarene began.

A. An Old Testament Worship Background

The Hebrews were a worshiping people. Worship was a powerful force in the life of a loyal Hebrew. For nearly 15 centuries prophets, priests, and kings hammered out a Jewish history in which the worship of Jehovah formed a central element in both public and private thought.

It was the Old Testament priests, however, who exercised so much control by acting as custodians over ceremonies, special day events, and so on. Andrew Blackwood notes the prominence of the priest in public worship, and Franklin Segler notes the priest as one who "played an important part in the system [of worship], for he dramatized the offering of sacrifices."[1] Hebrew religion was so structured that people came to accept priests as mediators through whom they met God. Ilion Jones states that the priests' energies

> were so consumed in detailed rites, rules, and rubrics pertaining to the sacred places, the observance of holy days and seasons, the handling of holy objects, the variety of practices such as sacrifices . . . the altar and its sacred vessels, the insense, the fires . . . which accompanied their conduct of worship.[2]

Thus priestly power served to dominate much of public worship.

But Old Testament prophets taught that God is "actually displeased with all acts of worship which are mere formalities unrelated to ethical living."[3] In an effort to reduce formality and ritualism in public worship, Amos, Hosea, Micah, Isaiah, and others focused their ministry on heart purity. Jones suggests that Hosea was "the first prophet to hint at a purely prayer worship as distinct from sacrifice worship . . . implying that God prefers the offering of prayers to the offering of material sacrifices."[4]

Thus prophets saw worship, eventually, as a way to honor God for His mercy, not merely as an expression of human methodology. Offerings of blood, food, vegetables, and animals were common. The prophets did not condemn sacrifice per se but abhorred dependence upon ritual to the exclusion of true heart and life change. As the worship practice of sacrifice rose in prominence during the first 800 years of Old Testament history, "the moral laws of God were forgotten or ignored by the priests."[5] Worship was performance, at times a pagan practice. Of course, not only was this a fallen world, it was a world without the redemptive knowledge of Jesus Christ.

Praise as an expression of worship may be seen in the use of Davidic psalms for singing. Often called the Hymn-book of Israel, the Psalms "were used expressly for public worship on special occasions or for the celebration of particular events."[6] This prompted the involvement of common people in singing, prayer, and personal devotion, and later proved useful for New Testament worship. Such direct communication with God, as opposed to going through a priest, "prepared the way for the New Testament doctrine of the priesthood of all believers."[7]

Thus as music, public prayer, and scripture reading were practiced by the laity in worship, "learning was no longer confined to the professional priestly elite. All people were taught to listen, to understand, to discuss, to reason."[8] As the laity emerged, even in Old Testament worship practice, freedom of involvement developed. Both priest and prophet labored together in leading worship. While ritualism did not die a sudden death, at least worshipers were seeing the meaning of true heart worship. The stage was set, finally, for community worship among new Christians in the rising New Testament period of the Early Church.

B. Worship Among the Early Christians During the New Testament Period

The most significant influence upon early Christian worship was the synagogue, for here Jews received both devotional and educational instruction. When the Temple was destroyed in A.D. 70 and the Church dispersed from Jerusalem to all parts of the world, synagogues became the pattern for Jewish worship activity. Eventually, the Christian Church modeled itself after the synagogue and not the Temple, which signaled an emphasis upon the Word and not upon sacrifice during worship. William Willimon, adjunct professor of worship and liturgy at Duke Divinity School, Greenville, S.C., suggests that "there is little doubt of the great influence of the form and content of synagogue worship in general on the liturgical life of the early church."[9]

Not all of the customs, practices, and methods of Old Testament worship changed as the New Testament period began. Willimon notes that before early Christians were Christians they were Jews. There were centuries of powerful influence from Israel's history. This fact could not then, and must not today, be discounted. The Jews were a deeply religious people with time-honored worship habits and memories. So it is fair to say that the New Testament Church did not abandon the Temple and all that it stood for any more than Diaspora Judaism did. Certainly with the destruction of the Temple and the shift away from blood sacrifice came many innovations. The people *were* involved in worship. The words of both Old and New Testament prophets *did* carry weight. But the single most historical fact that affected not only worship but the worshiper was the conviction that Jesus was the Messiah! Surely the eschatological age of the Spirit had burst upon them, and this itself gave a new freedom and power in corporate worship life. As Ralph Martin writes, "Christians of the apostolic era were conscious of living in days of eschatological fulfillment."[10] Simply put, Christ was alive and among His people! Methods of giving praise and attributing worth to God took on dimensions unique to a people caught up in the reality that Christ the Messiah had come!

The Old Testament custom of Temple worship continued as an influence upon New Testament worshipers. Segler observes that "the earliest Christians were . . . faithful in their worship at the temple . . . and made constant use of Jewish liturgical forms."[11] But as Christ emerged in witness, Segler suggests that the Christians "no longer needed the temple in Jerusalem, for Christ himself had become their Temple, their place for meeting God in worship."[12]

The language and fervor of prayers, for early Christians, though often traditional, were not the lifeless mouthings prevalent just years prior. New Testament worshipers of God in Christ knew the Messiah had come. Even the language of prayer changed! "We must believe that some of [their prayers] were free, spontaneous . . . and not vain repetitions of the sort condemned by the Master."[13] Ralph Martin suggests that Paul's prayers were not commonplace in language, but reflected "the liturgical life of the Churches."[14] Church worship was not only prayerful, but was rich and orderly in the truest sense of worshipful devotion.

Another worship activity which continued from Judaism was the regular contributions of tithes and offerings. Paul's word to the Corinthian church was: "Every Sunday each of you is to put aside and keep by him a sum in proportion to his gains" (1 Cor. 16:2, NEB). He recognized the legal duty of tithing as a good Jew. In New Testament life, "Money which had been honestly gained in the toil of the week [was] to be brought to the assembly of the church and thus made a part of the Sunday worship."[15]

As the church developed, a new spirit of spontaneity among the Christians grew and is captured by Segler: "There was a spirit of zeal in Christian worship produced by the consciousness that the Holy Spirit had come to make Christ regnant in their midst."[16] This kind of contagious enthusiasm, coupled with persecution, edged the Early Church out of the four walls of the synagogues and into homes. Not that Christians repudiated church buildings, but there were simply no established meeting places at first. The use of "house churches" became popular. From about the third century onward, Christians began to build structures for church services.[17]

Perhaps the new unity among new Christians, both Jew

27

and Gentile, is often overlooked. In reality, what we observe is a togetherness, a commonly felt bond that was expressed even in gathering for worship. The glue that seemed to hold together this surging, daring, and, yes, even timid band of believers was their commitment to Jehovah. His Son was among them! Getting together for Sabbath worship was an event. James F. White, a leading authority on worship and recently appointed professor of liturgy at the University of Notre Dame, South Bend, Ind., writes, "The importance of meeting or coming together can hardly be overstated. At times, the Jewish term 'synagogue' (coming together) was also used for the Christian assembly (James 2:2)."[18] Since the days of the Early Church, Christians have found a sense of identity and unity that comes from meeting for worship. No doubt this added to the sense of mutual fellowship:

> The enthusiasm, the spontaneous outburst of spiritual power, put new vitality into their singing, their prayers, their giving, their preaching, their testimony. . . . It was this that put "life" into New Testament worship . . . and that distinguished it from other types of worship.[19]

It is fair to say, then, that worship was a proclamation not only of what happened, but what was currently happening in their lives as the Holy Spirit brought renewed freshness to them.

C. The Influence of the Reformation During the Rise of Protestantism

During the Middle Ages (about A.D. 500 to 1500) worship appears to have lost its vitality. Many Christians died for their faith. Others renounced the faith. While Reformers such as Huss and Wycliffe fought to keep alive the sparks of evangelism, national, religious, and political leaders fostered pagan ideologies which weakened the church. For new Christians, the effect was deadening. Moreover, the distinction between a power-hungry clergy and a drifting laity sharpened:

> Unevangelical doctrine perverted spiritual worship. . . . With the increase of material power and form of the Church, unworthy men sought her offices. . . . Religion became an outward ceremony apart from the character and the life. A people thus trained had no hunger for the Word and the Church no message to give, and the sermon became a small incident of the service and at last generally given up. The worship expanded into an imposing dramatic and symbolic ritual.[20]

Several crucial theological errors heightened the problem during the Middle Ages prior to the Reformation: (1) The priest mediated between God and the people; (2) priests supposedly had power to change the bread and wine of the sacrament into the body and blood of Christ; (3) priests offered the sacrifice of the mass for the sins of the living and dead; and (4) priests were given power to forgive sins.[21] As the political and ecclesiastical power of the church rose, its social voice declined. As the clergy gained autocratic power, the laity lost their influence, witness, and interest.

Into this atmosphere of confusion and departure from New Testament theology came the Reformers, men whose preaching, teaching, and writing created the Reformation. The Reformation was a religious revolution of the 16th and 17th centuries which divided the Western church into Protestantism and Roman Catholicism. These protester-reformers were in the vanguard of Protestantism. These men simply wanted to restore the people's right to sound biblical theology and worship forms.

The influence of *Martin Luther (1483-1546)* in Germany was awesome. Called the Divine Helper of Protestantism, Luther opposed dramatic worship change and papal domination of the church. His value of preaching invited the wrath of the established Catholic church. Blackburn, Hoyt, Phifer, Billington, and other scholars and liturgical historians stress the value Luther gave the sermon.

Luther's commitment to the priesthood of all believers paved the way for the laity to express gifts and ministries, as is seen in his attitude toward hymnology. Luther wrote many hymns (including "A Mighty Fortress Is Our God") and encouraged others to write for the church. Luther strongly favored congregational singing. "One of the famous Theses Martin Luther nailed to the great door of the Wittenburg Church was his plea for congregational singing, the demand that laymen be given the right to sing hymns as a part of worship."[22]

The Reformation influenced Switzerland under *Ulrich Zwingli (1484-1531).* Zwingli tried to abolish music during public worship, having destroyed 10 church organs in Zurich, Switzerland, alone. "One of his most radical changes was to discontinue use of the organ and abolish congregational singing for which he substituted the antiphonal recitation of psalms and canticles."[23] S. F. Winward is more critical of Zwingli: "The baneful influence of Zwingli, who at Zurich, excluded singing, banished common prayer, reduced the congregation to silence, and turned the whole of Sunday 'preaching service' into a ministerial dialogue, has been widespread."[24] He denounced lay leadership in the church.

Luther and Zwingli did agree on the major issues dividing the Reformers from Rome. J. S. Whale notes that the "superiority of Scripture to ecclesiastical authority, justification by faith, and the priesthood of all believers"[25] were areas where Luther and Zwingli were at one. Zwingli also served the Lord's Supper less often than Luther, and originated the custom of "sitting Communion" in which worshipers were served by deacons as they remained in their pews.[26]

John Calvin's (1509-64) influence was felt largely in France. The product of a very religious home, Calvin's attitudes toward the high value of preaching are felt to this day. Kenneth Phifer notes that "although Luther restored preaching to a central place in the worship experience of the church, it was left to the Zwingli-Bucer-Calvin school to exalt it to preeminence."[27]

In worship, Calvin used the Psalms for music because they were Scripture, and he was largely suspicious of other music, particularly instrumental music. "Calvin could not abide the use of instruments . . . [largely because] of their association with pagan religions and with the licentious life of the pagan around them, and partly [due] to the distrust of the sensuous impressions aroused by music."[28]

Thus the Reformers sought to free the church of priestly domination, abolished the selling of indulgences and penance, converted the use of the altar to facilitate Communion, lifted the significance of preaching and congregational singing, and reestablished the voice and involvement of the laity in liturgy. But it was John and Charles Wesley who continued the Reformation many years later in England and Scotland that so greatly influenced worship practices for Methodists and Nazarenes.

D. The Wesleys: Their Influence in England in the 1700s and 1800s, and the Development of Methodism on the American Frontier

1. England in the 1700s and 1800s: "The Reformation in England and Scotland was inspired by triumphant singing . . . [and] the great Wesleyan movement thrilled the heart of England by its more intimate preaching and hymn singing."[29] Some 200 years after the Reformation in Germany, Switzerland, France, and England came the English Evangelical Revival, largely through the efforts of *John (1703-91) and*

Charles Wesley (1707-88), sons of the noted Church of England parsonage in Epworth, Lincolnshire.

Charles was the author of some 6,500 hymns, while John flamed the hearts of the English with his intimate field preaching. Fiske suggests that "it may be questioned whether John Wesley's inspired preaching or his brother's inspired music was the major influence in that great spiritual revolution of the eighteenth century."[30] Our attention will be given to both men as they brought light to both the theology and hymnology of the church. Wesleyan theology and doctrine culminated in the founding of Methodism and is the theological root system for the Church of the Nazarene.

Before the spread of Methodism to the United States, England witnessed the development of Wesley's small-group class meetings, one of many new church-life innovations. An Anglican (Church of England), Wesley encouraged his supporters to attend Sunday worship in the Anglican church. While he is credited for founding Methodism, Wesley still loved his own church. Harry Emerson Fosdick wrote, "Wesley himself never ceased being a High Church Episcopalian."[31] The Methodist Episcopal church, a branch of Methodism, became established in the United States. But Wesley brought to Methodism a mix of Anglican decorum and typically Wesleyan spontaneity.

Perhaps Wesley's worship perspective for Methodists is best summed up by Horton Davies, who quotes F. C. Gill, editor of *Selected Letters of John Wesley.* Wesley desired these worship components:

> There are six in all: a simple, undistracting setting for worship which is neither too elegant nor too rude; the social homogeneity of the worshipers and their sincerity; the solemnity and integrity of the one conducting Divine worship; the singing, which combines sense and poetry in the hymnody and vigor in the rendering; the preaching, which is a plain,

earnest proclamation of the gospel of a present salvation by a man whose life adorns his doctrine; and the Communion celebrated by a worthy minister to a holy people.[32]

Music was a significant element in Wesleyan worship. Both Wesley brothers wrote hymns and encouraged congregational singing. Raymond Abba parallels Free church and Anglican worship:

> In the Anglican tradition the use of hymns is normally limited to supplying the opening and closing praise of worship; in Free Church services, they may also voice the corporate prayer of the congregation and express their confession of faith. The chief function of a hymn is to be the expression of a church's praise.[33]

Thus Davies concludes that "Wesley found Anglican praise seriously wanting and considered Methodist praise much superior. . . . [Wesley's] Methodist worshipers sing their praise with the heart . . . [they] do not sit and sing, they stand and praise God 'lustily and with good courage.'"[34] We are able to see that Wesley's music encouraged liveliness and congregational participation, giving "free expression to the warmth of the religious emotions."[35] Already we are able to see the link between early Wesleyan worship and our worship practice as Nazarenes. But it is noteworthy that "the singing of hymns by the congregation in the modern sense did not begin until the eighteenth century during the Wesleyan revival."[36]

But music was not the only significant change. Wesley was to see the development of Methodist "preaching houses" as a major pivotal issue in the loss of many members from the Church of England. He did not desire division within the Anglican church; yet proliferation of preaching houses where the worship was spontaneous, the singing was exciting, the preaching was intimate, all contributed to structural change. The secure Church of England was not able to hold people who had tasted the new wine of more informal worship.

It was the development of "societies" which influenced the worshiping style of Methodism. Societies were groups of worshipers who were subdivided into "classes" and further into "bands." "Several 'bands' or 'classes' made up a 'society' and within these fractional communities there developed a special expression of group worship."[37] While not the original invention of Wesley (but of the Moravians) these small groups helped initiate the Methodist movement in England. Worship in these groups included fasting and frequent Communion. Wesley "provided in the Class and Band meetings a means of close fellowship and mutual help, and a homely ministry of confession and reconciliation."[38]

Thus extemporary prayers, warmhearted singing, intimate preaching (often done outdoors), and small-group fellowship meetings were factors that awakened Wesley's England and quickened a sense of congregational revitalization. Revival had come! And as Methodism came to America, it certainly influenced the pioneer spirit of that country which was ready for a religious awakening.

2. Methodism on the American Frontier: The small groups formed the character for worship renewal in America, finally, with the surge of "love feasts," "covenant services," "watch night services," and "prayer meetings." Not all of Wesley's liturgical methods took root in American soil, but the love feasts did, partly to the credit of Francis Asbury, one of Wesley's first helpers. Also, the covenant service, a time of personal examination of commitment, became established in America. John Bishop states that "it may be claimed that Methodism has contributed nothing more notable to the worship of the Church than the Covenant Service."[39]

Both the frontier spirit of anti-institutionalism in America and the spirit of spontaneity from Wesley produced an interesting worship climate. Bishop notes that "in America these services were . . . unstructured."[40] Extemporaneous (without notes) preaching, a marked decrease in the frequency of Communion (from weekly to monthly), and the introduction of testimonies were factors that encouraged a simpler form of worship service in America.

There need be no doubt that such an atmosphere fostered camp meeting life in young America. Perhaps Wesley's interest in spirited congregational music fanned the flame of camp meeting singing. Wesley wrote in *Sacred Melody:*

> Sing lustily and with good courage. Beware of singing as if you were half dead or half asleep, but lift up your voice with strength. . . . Sing modestly. Do not bawl, so as to be heard above or distinct from the rest of the congregation, that you may not destroy the harmony.[41]

Methodism made strong impressions upon the American frontier through camp meeting life. Worship could not be contained in church buildings, and the development of the camp meeting trail influenced evangelical worship in its formative years. Peter Cartwright was a preacher typical of many who either filled primitive Methodist pulpits or traveled the sawdust trail of camp meetings. Apropos of Cartwright, Sidney Mead sums up:

> The great mass of our western people wanted a preacher that could mount a stump, a block, or an old log, or stand in the bed of a wagon, and without note or manuscript, quote, expound, and apply the Word of God to the hearts and consciences of the people.[42]

Camp meeting life was as rough and tumble as the era that prevailed. In fact, for many illiterate people it became an informal religious "school," and a worship center for the spiritually hungry.

> Camp meeting combined praying, preaching, and singing, all in large and robust doses . . . The feeling of oneness of a congregation was only come by when the heterogeneous

crowd was caught up in an emotional ecstasy through the power of some masterful preacher or the ardor of some frontier hymn. . . . Frontier worship was crude and direct. . . . Worship was less an act of praise and renewal by the church . . . than it was a method of propagandizing for the purpose of converting the unconverted.[43]

We see, then, that the shift in ecclesiology from the small, intimate class meeting (such as the Wesleys') to the large camp meeting has helped to make legitimate both evangelism and "spectatorism" in congregational worship. A class meeting was where one participated, opened his soul, told his story. The camp meeting without question had its opportunity for participation, but its very nature demanded that one observe the music and preaching. The camp meeting was a place where something always happened, and folks wanted to be there to see it.

Stemming directly from rugged camp meeting life was revivalism. Of course, these fed one another. But worship in the local church in the 19th and 20th centuries reflected camp meeting flavor in many of its forms. Charles G. Finney, often called the Father of Modern Revivalism, was one of the many revivalists whose services colored public worship in the early days of Methodism in the United States. Donald Dayton says that "he popularized the 'protracted meeting' . . . and employed the 'anxious bench,' a row of seats in the front of the church for those under 'conviction' of sin."[44] From the anxious bench and use of the mourner's bench or altar rail, continues the use of the altar in our churches today. Even architecturally, Wesley argued for simplicity so that worshipers would not feel left out, and he opposed selling seats: " 'Let all our churches be built plain and decent, and with free seats.' "[45] Thus the ruggedness of camp meeting affected both style and symbolism in church worship.

Charles Jones offers that "where freelance revivalism met with early and sustained successes, the primary attraction seems to have been the nostalgic quality of holiness preaching and worship."[46] Perhaps this is evident from both the preaching of the fontiersmen as well as the popularity of so many Wesleyan hymns in America. Ernest Stoeffler affirms this:

> The heart-warming, Christ-oriented piety of Charles [Wesley] was highly treasured among the people called Methodists. This was true in America and is evident from the great number of such Christocentric hymns in the early American hymnals. . . . [His hymns] are at least partly responsible for Methodism's appeal to the people at the frontier.[47]

One of the new voices which appeared near the end of frontier America was a denomination of Wesleyan persuasion known as the Church of the Nazarene. The people called Nazarenes were dramatically affected by and were a part of Methodism as it was developed toward the conclusion of the 19th century.

E. Corporate Worship During the Early Days of the Church of the Nazarene

Originating in 1908, in Pilot Point, Tex., from the merging of several holiness bodies, the Church of the Nazarene today is the largest of church groups that preach entire sanctification. With a heritage in the perfectionist persuasion that stems from early Methodism, the Nazarenes were influenced by camp meeting life and revivalism that flourished at the close of the 19th century. While abundant resources regarding early Nazarene worship are scarce, we know that our roots were not in the "high church" tradition often found in the more formal worship practices of many liturgical churches.

Research by this writer, of original documents such as early issues of the *Herald of Holiness* and *Proceedings of the General Assembly* at the Nazarene Archives, reveals that while early Nazarenes did not have a formal written liturgy

37

or even a stated theology of worship, they still worshiped and had a worship theology. We will see that our worship style was greatly influenced by camp meeting life and revivalism, which, 100 years ago, was the early landmark of holiness evangelism. Dr. Hugh C. Benner, former general superintendent for the Nazarenes, made this statement about our worship in his 1954 dedication address of Nazarene Theological Seminary:

> To an amazing degree, early Nazarenes followed the spiritual pattern of the Church of Pentecost . . . Thus it is in this realm of the Spirit that we find the essence and genius of the Church of the Nazarene. Early Nazarenes were fervent in prayer, fervent in testimony, fervent in soul winning, and fervent in preaching. They were characterized by a spirit of spiritual freedom, both in worship and in service.[48]

This "essence and genius" was surely portrayed in the first Church of the Nazarene of Los Angeles, whose pastor was Dr. Phineas F. Bresee. Their building, called the "Glory Barn," was the scene of many a worship service upon which "the glory fell"—an expression common in our heritage. Mendell Taylor cites such a service (about 1898) in *The Nazarene Messenger:*

> The happy congregation(s) . . . are allowed an unrestrained freedom, which they use with encouragement from their leader. They laugh, clap their hands, shout "Amen" or "Hallelujah," walk to and fro, and one time we saw a colored sister execute in her joy the most beautiful dance we ever beheld. *It is not disorderly to "demonstrate" in a natural way the gladness of the heart in the Nazarene church* [italics mine].[49]

This same spirit is found in other places as the young denomination grew. Following are several accounts of church and revival services, camp meetings, and district assemblies as recorded in early issues of the *Herald of Holiness,* the official publication of the Church of the Nazarene:

Chicago, 1912: Last Sabbath was a great day. . . . A number of seekers prayed through to victory. One man literally ran to the altar. A lady started to the altar but fell in the aisle.[50]

Blossom, Tex., 1912: Such singing, testifying, praying, and shouting as is never known only when the Spirit of Pentecost prevails.[51]

Chicago, 1912: Large attendance this morning; folks laughing, crying, shouting joyful praises unto the Lord. Street march for Jesus today at 6:30 p.m. Usually one to two blocks long.[52]

Chicago, 1912: The ceremonies of the laying of the corner-stone occurred in the afternoon. The assembly gathered at the tent and formed a procession and marched to the church. . . . There was a fine band to lead with inspiring music and the organization and order was perfect. . . . The ceremony . . . was very informal but impressive. The meeting was full of enthusiasm.[53]

Southern California Camp Meeting, 1945: There were about 800 seekers at the altar, with many happy finders. . . . [There were] shouts of joy rising from the hearts of the saints.[54]

Dallas District Assembly, 1945: Waves of glory swept over the capacity audience, and prolonged shouting marked the unusual outpouring of God's Spirit upon His people.[55]

New Galilee, Pa., 1908 (from the *Beulah Christian*): (church dedication service) The praise service in the evening was glorious, and the saints wept, laughed, shouted, and praised the Lord till it was difficult to stop them for the dedicatory service . . . The service was concluded about 9:00 p.m. with the Doxology . . . and how the people did shout! . . . sinners were converted, backsliders reclaimed, and believers were sanctified on up until about 11:00 p.m.[56]

Thus Nazarenes worshiped—or even more accurately, celebrated! For these were a group of folks who met to praise God for His goodness among them. It is as if they could not help but rejoice!

As the Nazarenes merged, camp meeting life had already affected them and would continue to do so. The significance of social and moral reform fostered by revivalism and camp

39

meetings cannot be overlooked, in spite of the seemingly excessive demonstration that accompanied this era:

> Great crowds would attend these meetings. People would work hard all day and go to meeting at night to hear them sing and shout. Great power was upon the people, and oftentimes while the preacher was preaching people would take the jerks, or fall off their seats into the straw, screaming for mercy, and when the altar call was made they would run to the altar, weeping as they went, and such praying around the altar you seldom hear.[57]

This was neither the custom nor an oddity among people from various types of religious groups. It seems to have been part of the flavor of church life among both fundamentalists and some of the holiness persuasion to express emotional reaction in varied, nearly uninhibited manners.

The public expression of emotions is further borne out by accounts of our early General Assemblies as the Church of the Nazarene assumed organizational structure. Beginning with the 1907 General Assembly, the reader will note that worship takes the form of freedom and spontaneity in music, honoring the sacraments, and participation in love feasts. Nazarenes did not have any recorded Sunday services at their first three General Assemblies.

> *First General Assembly, 1907:* It was thought wise to occupy the morning ... of the first day with preparatory services of prayer and the Sacrament of the Lord's Supper. ... The whole company joined in singing "March On, We Shall Win the Day," amid shouts, waving the handkerchiefs and general hearty greetings all around. It was with difficulty that Dr. Bresee brought the Assembly into enough calmness to continue business, so great was the enthusiasm. ... In the singing ... so filled were they with holy joy that for many minutes it was impossible to restrain it.[58]

> *Second General Assembly, 1908:* The burst of holy joy continued for several minutes. ... Soon the inside of the tent became too small for the freedom of such joy, and the people began marching out and around the great tent, with waving

handkerchiefs and shouts of joy, and eventually formed in an immense solid circle on the grounds, where Dr. Bresee mounted a chair and addressed the multitude.[59]

Fourth General Assembly, 1915: (First recorded *Sunday* service) . . . The bread and water was passed and the people of God partook together . . . Many joined in giving words of testimony to the joys of salvation. . . . The "love feast" closed with the singing of the Doxology.

Evening Service: . . . The text of the evening was "Grieve not the Spirit." *Great silence brooded over the congregation during the presentation of the truth.* About thirty persons sought the Lord at this service [italics mine].[60]

Mendell Taylor observes, with regard to elements in Nazarene worship, that "the Church of the Nazarene has no fixed mode of baptism nor order for the Sacrament of the Lord's Supper. . . . The primary emphasis is on the relationship the worshiper has with the Lord, rather than any ceremony he engaged in."[61]

Thus our worship history developed from centuries of priestly domination to prophetic warnings, from Holy Spirit movings to medieval persecution, from Reformation in Europe to revival in America. To distill the best of history's lessons while preserving our heritage, the Church of the Nazarene

must declare a distinctive doctrine ("holiness unto the Lord"), *it must maintain a distinctive spirit with a climate of freedom and spontaneity* . . . and it must emphasize a distinctive discipline to show that the Lordship of Christ makes a world of difference [italics mine].[62]

And the task before us now, some 75 years into our journey, is to do it in a world compounded with ease, cynicism, and distorted worship perspectives. Our next chapter will enable us to reflect upon our heritage as we deal with tensions affecting our worship.

3

Predicament

Tensions Affecting
Our Worship Today

"Oh, What Needless Pain We Bear"

The previous chapter has shown not only the place of Nazarene worship within the whole of Christian liturgy, but the pattern of spontaneity so evident in our early days.

We are blessed with a heritage deeply rooted in the soil of heartfelt, old-time religion. And that religion is most commonly expressed during our church services. W. T. Purkiser, in *Called unto Holiness* (vol. 2), cites seven fundamental characteristics of the Church of the Nazarene as delivered by General Superintendent J. W. Goodwin in his Quadrennial Address to the 1932 General Assembly. The sixth-mentioned characteristic by Goodwin is as follows:

> Spiritual freedom, a "simplicity of Pentecostal worship," has characterized the church from its beginning. People are attracted and held by "joyous freedom in the ministry of the Word and the glad testimonies of saving grace" which alone can assure the permanency of the movement as a spiritual force.[1]

Evidence thus abounds related to the "showers of bless-ing" Nazarenes have enjoyed in their worship settings. Why, then, speak of tensions? After all, don't we still sing the great hymns of the faith, enjoy a happy spirit of spontaneity resulting in testimonies of the saints, celebrate the sacraments, receive offerings from faithful givers, preach the ageless message of full salvation, extend altar calls, and get home in time for dinner? And Nazarenes enjoy this privilege twice on Sunday when many denominations meet only once. What tensions could possibly affect such effort?

It will be helpful in assessing the local church situation to not be critical of worship customs, traditions, or styles. The important issue before us will be to appraise honestly our current worship life in light of problems which distort and cloud worship. While we cannot deny that there are misperceptions and tensions in our worship, these may be dealt with more reasonably if we determine the trends in our society today that affect Christian liturgy.

In the early 1930s when Goodwin made his statement to the General Assembly, he was reflecting upon his day. It would be simplistic to say that he spoke of an easy, problem-free world where people had no worries and worship was never influenced adversely by evil. That was not the case, for then the United States was in the throes of severe economic depression, and the clouds of yet another world war hung heavy.

Fifty years ago the young Nazarene church still had many living witnesses from the 1908 Pilot Point merger, and our mission as a church was very distinct. Moreover, the secular world knew the position of the church world, and there was little mistake in the minds of anyone which was which. Worship, too, among Nazarenes in the 30s was not only a reflection of mission stated but mission accomplished in an age less cluttered with national cynicism and moral ambiguity.

I agree with Nazarene elder Gene Van Note, author of *The People Called Nazarenes,* who observes that in our early days it *was* easier to define and fulfill our mission than it is today. He speaks of the unlikely possibility that "average" Nazarenes today would be able to articulate our mission—spreading scriptural holiness across the land—as simply and directly as did our forebears:

> This is not necessarily cynical. Language changes. Words become popular and then fade into the musty depths of the unabridged dictionary. Increased levels of education and sophistication change the way a person views his world and how its ills can be healed. . . . *[T]he church must be flexible enough to minister the eternal Word of God to its own day.* If it is not able to do that successfully, it will become the vestigial remnant of some bygone dream [italics mine].[2]

There can be little doubt that both society and the church are vastly different now compared to a half century ago. Times were hard then, but distinctions were clear. Times are hard now, but distinctions are much more difficult to assess. Thus in an age of conflicting and confusing issues, the church has the task of remaining a reliable and credible witness. Interpreting our mission today demands of this generation the willingness to respond to the subtle trends and influences of the secular world. We cannot automatically assume that inner contentment assures or indicates healthy life within the church.

The issue before us is not that of changing worship styles to meet the age of high tech. Our task is to be so perceptive of changing world conditions that we may recognize the church's failure to accomplish its mission. Otherwise, the world will quite easily blind the church and cause it to misjudge its mission, its achievement, and its reason for existence. Public worship is the occasion when we may interpret effectively both the feelings of our hearts and the convictions of sound biblical theology. The Nazarene worship service, with its vibrant singing, free spirit, and expositional preaching, is the proving grounds for this to be accomplished. Most definitely then, the worship hour cannot be seen as the refuge in which to hide from worldly influence. For it may be the very place where worldly influence is waging its strongest battle.

As we enter the closing years of the 20th century, it is my conviction that several factors are creating dilemmas for the church which were not necessarily common to our forefathers. Among these are (1) ambiguity in the definition of worship; (2) the increasing popularity of the church in the world and the world in the church; (3) lack of clarity related to the expression of our emotions and spontaneity; (4) the rise of a performance-spectator mentality; (5) a vague biblical and historical perspective; and (6) the ultimate tendency toward pastoral control and the subsequent paralysis of lay ministry in worship renewal.

Such issues, if unresolved, lead to confusion and misunderstanding related to congregational worship. Let us observe three major tensions facing our worship today in order to determine an appropriate Christian response.

Fascination: Our Flare for the Fantastic

I remember the novel and fantastic in worship. What wiggly preacher's kid wouldn't? Sunday School contests whose grand finale was cutting off the necktie or breaking a record over the head of the losing team leader by the winning leader, numerous skits and attention-getting programs, various musical groups and traveling evangelists who sang and told their stories, prizes awarded, and goldfish swallowed—these and other colorful features filled my childhood and youthful memories. And if they did not entertain me, I entertained myself as a child by discovering that the man who sat behind Mother and me during worship wore a wooden leg which he kept propped up on the pew.

Once a converted penitentiary inmate visited on a Sunday morning, dressed in his black and white, wide-striped prison garb. Bill Mills brought his own electric chair and preached on God's righteousness while sitting in it. Since I waited the whole service to see what would happen, I didn't remember the sermon. But I never forgot the chair.

These long-cherished memories provided the flavor of another day (not that they are all that uncommon today), a flavor that somehow enriched, taught, and made spontaneous our services. I have never begrudged the spirit in which they were presented nor my memory of them.

As time has passed, however, we have largely eliminated many of the more colorful and novel activities from worship services. Perhaps we feel we do not need them now. But we may have substituted their presence for a loosely defined folk theology whose focus features novelty in yet other ways. It seems, sometimes, that we have the capacity to make legitimate every aspect of religion during our worship except the one item most needed of all: worship itself.

For some time now we have been caught up—fascinated—with our flare for the fantastic. It has certainly not been done in a spirit of disrespect for the meaning of worship, but perhaps indicates a searching for ways to honor our relationship with God. Don M. Wardlaw, professor of preaching and worship at McCormick Theological Seminary, makes this observation:

> [W]here does holy irrelevance have its rightful place in worship? . . . we are simply asking in a multitude of ways what worship is. We are admitting amid the tensions at the worship hour that many of us have delayed too long in comprehending the richness and majesty of our praises.[3]

And in our search for a worship identity, for worship meaning and significance, we have missed something of the grandeur of the event itself. For the special tension created is that the things which tend to fascinate us may also be the things that tend to detract us from our purpose as worshipers. Let us look briefly, then, at our reason for meeting in the worship hour.

Clarity in our definition and purpose of worship is the beginning point. Worship is simply giving worth to God and ascribing praise to Him for who He is. It is giving glory to God for His majesty, His power, and His divine nature. Certainly we thank God for His goodness to us. But a fine distinction between thanksgiving and praise is that we thank God for what He does for us, but we praise Him for who He is. If worship is only a thanksgiving time for the blessings we have been given, then the focus is at least partly on us. Certainly worship is gratitude. It is also confession and supplication. But the neglected aspect of our worship is that of lifting up and magnifying the greatness of God just because He is God!

The vital elements of adoration, confession, thanksgiving, and supplication are all necessary to true worship. Each must find a place in the Christian worship service. We may sing, speak, listen, observe, laugh, shout, cry, or give money during worship, but these will remain as merely human responses unless God is honored in them. In fact, our human activity may help *us;* it may be even therapeutic in the sense that any emotional release is healthy. But to allow ourselves to become fascinated with spectacular activity, however credible or interesting, is not worshipful if it does not help us give glory to the Father. In an article titled "Worship as the Recognition of the Holy," cited in the *Preacher's Magazine,* General Superintendent William Greathouse takes note of William Temple's perspective on worship purpose:

> To worship is to quicken the conscience by the holiness of God, to feed the mind on the truth of God, to purge the imagination by the beauty of God, to open the heart to the love of God, to devote the will to the purpose of God.[4]

Thus the definition of worship seems clear. The day may be coming to an end in many places, where novelty will be defined only in terms of promotional technique. But a more subtle and theologically sophisticated fascination is now before us that may distort our understanding of worship. It is that of subjectivism, a kind of self-focus in which we capitalize upon our blessings and our experiences. For this is most definitely an age of experience-centered religion.

The subtle influence of experience-centered religion in which we see what God has done for us more than we see God, may remove the keen edge of our perception of God's holiness from our worship, thus magnifying personal experience. As Greathouse states,

> To object that we have not been affected by this mood of our time is to be deliberately blind. Our religious culture is suffering an eclipse of the Transcendent, that which Rudolph Otto calls "the Holy." The God who at one time may have been too much the "Wholly Other" is now almost entirely "One of us."[5]

The mood this creates may be both disrespect for and denial of God, plus that of showing such casual reverence and awe for His holiness that our perception of Him is cheapened. If we cannot overcome the snare of self-centeredness, the One who is to be worshiped pales in significance by our attempts at self-reward. Samuel Miller, in *The Life of the Soul,* sums it up:

> There is little chance of recovering the sense of reality in the worship of God unless there is some living capacity for wonder and awe in the hearts of those who come to church. Without this, worship will be degraded by attempts to make it interesting, novel, even fantastic.[6]

This comes into sharp focus for evangelicals and particularly those of the perfectionist persuasion as it relates to the occurrence of evangelism during worship. Under a chapter titled "Nazarene Self-image in 1933," in Purkiser's previously cited work, he observes:

> A rather typical pattern had developed in which the morning worship hour on Sunday was usually given to some aspect of the doctrine, experience or life of holiness. . . . By tradition, the Sunday evening service was the "evangelistic service" of the week.[7]

While holiness has been the mainstay of our preaching, it is interesting to note that, at least in recent years, we have made the morning worship service more evangelistic because so many of the unsaved attend then. We may sing hymns of worship, but we have necessarily preached the gospel message and given altar calls. Sunday night has continued to be more informal, especially in our singing, testimonies, and order of service. Certainly the holiness message is preached in either service.

It is important to ask, in light of the fact that evangelism and worship have been so synonymous in our past, "When *do* we worship?" and "In what way will we worship when we actually come to evangelize and teach?"

Nazarenes are a unique people in a unique time in history. It is very difficult to define, in general terms that fit all of us, how we are worshiping. But most Nazarenes attend services that are evangelistic and informal both Sunday morning and night. There are exceptions, but, compared to the more liturgical churches, we are not formal. It is probably helpful for us to see that when a preacher evangelizes from the pulpit, he is honoring God; and when a sinner surrenders at an altar of prayer, he, too, is giving worth to God. Confessing the Lordship of Christ is a form of giving praise to the Father.

But worship must occur even if evangelism does not. Even if there are no seekers at the altar, even if there is no mighty spirit of conviction, the worth and praise given to God must still happen. And we must see that if evangelism takes place we must still worship! The fact that a given worshiper is already saved must not prevent him from worshiping God in a service where evangelism is the theme. It is so important for us to understand in our minds that evangelism means the salvation of the lost—certainly a worthy experience confessing Christ's Lordship—and that worship includes so much more than that!

Evangelism and spontaneity are our style, to the praise and glory of God! But whether we have them in every service or not, God must still be praised because He is broader than any given "style." In other words, worship can occur in a service that is not evangelistic. Evangelism is surely a way Nazarenes are used to giving God the glory. But in services where there are no seekers we must not conclude that there was no praise given.

Let us forever enjoy the happy blend of evangelism that is mixed with freedom in the Spirit! But let us remember that worship is not a matter of style or mood, but a determination of the heart to ascribe to God the honor due His name.

Spectator Mentality:
The Worldliness of Religious Popularity
in an Age of Dirty Feet

Somewhere there is a concert hall. Or a church. Or a civic auditorium. People have paid good money to get in. The place is packed with those who have come to hear their favorite performer. The concert runs for 90 minutes. Sometimes there is hilarity. Always there is thunderous applause. Later, into the night, the crowds go home, the entertainers load up, and the lights are turned off. But next week, they will be back. Perhaps in a different place. Perhaps someone else will perform. And it will happen all over again. And across the street from the big event is a mother of four in a two-room flat with no money for electricity.

"You cannot make up scenarios," some say. And that is true. Everybody deserves a night at the concert. Good entertainment is hard to find. Christian performers are surely not to blame if people like their music. Nothing wrong with having stars to look up to. But all of that misses the point, for the reality is that Christian people everywhere are doing good things for good reasons in a world of dirty feet. Perhaps we cannot wash all the dirty feet around us, but we can certainly be aware of things we give our time and money to and the values we hold.

And we can be aware, too, that in a dangerously true sense, the Church is gaining respectability in the world and the world is gaining popularity in the Church. That is good because the Church is, hopefully, in position to influence the world, and it is bad because the world is too often popular with the Church.

This odd relationship has been a long time coming, for there was a time when the Church and world were, literally, worlds apart. But no more. And Christians, sensing the rise of religious popularity, have discovered that evangelism and evangelicalism are "in." Some may disagree, but not Jon Johnston, author of *Will Evangelicalism Survive Its Own Popularity?* He writes,

> In many ways the eighth decade of this century has been as good to the "born-againers" as the seventh one was to the war protesters. . . . In contrast to earlier periods, evangelicals are no longer equated with holy rollers, counterfeit preachers, simple-mindness, rampant hypocrisy, bad theology or poor taste.[8]

Johnston cites Martin Marty, renowned church historian, who discussed conditions within American society that may have prompted the evangelical renaissance, namely that "contemporary American culture no longer stigmatizes or persecutes the evangelical. Conversely, the born-againer has opportunity to prosper and gain social acceptance."[9] Further, Marty suggests that because society has failed in its attempt to provide belongingness, evangelicalism "offers a rite of passage for those seeking to come from a nondescript world to a world of acceptance and support."[10]

At issue here is whether the Church can remain a credible witness to the world or be drawn, instead, into the world's value system. If the Church looks to the world as its model of success, be it in entertainment or any other field, then the witness is lost. Timothy L. Smith in *Called unto Holiness* (vol. 1) cites the reason many Methodist preachers and laymen left that denomination in the 1920s. States Smith, these Methodists

> brought with them both the ideas and the attitudes of what we have called Wesleyan fundamentalism, including especially a deeply ingrained fear of ecclesiastical compromise, and an abhorrence of personal worldliness and fashionable forms of worship.[11]

Dean Inge offers the same concept in a note of prediction: "When the Church marries the spirit of the age, she will be left a widow in the next generation."[12] This is what Hoon referred to as the danger of the "secularization of our people's perceptions." And without the intention of unholy alliance, the church is suddenly in a vulnerable position.

The tension for the church is to remain a reliable witness by refusing to sacrifice its credibility to the god of worldly popularity. Failure to do so means accommodating a dubious value system within the protective custody of its mission. And it is within the sacred precincts of the church at worship that we may be most severely tested.

One of the obvious testing grounds is Christian music, where the blending of sacred and secular music is so subtly done that the differences between Christian praise and worldly entertainment are often confused if not indistinguishable. The response of the passive worshiper is often failure to distinguish between what is truly entertaining and

52

what is truly God-honoring. Entertainment *can* be God-honoring, but when is it? And when is it not? When does a "praise gathering" cease to be praise and become entertainment? If it can be both at the same time, then are we attending to be entertained or to give praise to God?

This is not much of an issue for people who attend a Saturday night concert at an auditorium and expect to be entertained. No doubt but that there can be much true worship and praise, too. But what about Sunday morning when we gather in church for the purpose of worship? Are we then, too, being entertained by the musicians or preacher? Or are we capable of worship? Are we more impressed with the performer, showmanship, and decibels than we are with the message of the words? When the concert is over or the singer/preacher sits down, do we leave saying, "What a fantastic singer!" or "I am moved to serve God by . . ."? To be impressed with the skill of the performer is certainly not wrong. But if the performer's skill clouds our view of God, something is certainly not right!

The focus we have in this age of entertainment must not be upon the medium but upon the message. Marshall McLuhan says the medium *is* the message. Perhaps that's our problem. The star, the music, the whole performance must not become greater than the *message* or meaning. If we are passive observers or spectators, our chances of missing the message are very high. The worshiper will simply need to distinguish between the human desire to be entertained and the need to hear and respond faithfully to the Christian message.

Theologian Søren Kierkegaard recognized an appropriate solution to this problem when he suggested that worship leaders serve as prompters of the audience who may be seen as the chief "actors" upon the stage or platform. The audience, as encouraged by the worship leaders, gave an expression of true praise to God, who sat alone in the large auditorium or sanctuary. As Greathouse declares, "Worship is not something done before or for the congregation, as if those leading are actors and the congregation an audience."[13] If the Christian world is unable or unwilling to overcome its spectator mentality, then we are doomed for increasing confusion and ambiguity regarding our purpose as worshipers. Richard Dinwiddie in "Moneychangers in the Church: Making the Sounds of Music," makes this observation:

> Confusion . . . has resulted from the familiar tension between ministry and entertainment. "Ministry" has itself become a code word that may or may not be taken at face value; it is sometimes a cover for the real, commercial motivation. Although we may enjoy the ministry of music, the primary purpose must not be entertainment. George Frideric Handel's classic statement in 1741 after the premiere of his *Messiah* is still valid: "Sir, I should be sorry if I only entertained them; I had hoped to make them better."[14]

Being made better has little, if anything, to do with whether or not we have a sense of fulfillment through Christian entertainment. But it has everything to do with a sense of fulfillment through servanthood. The sad consequence of passivity is the loss of servanthood for the fun of being a spectator. And in an age of Christian idols, fans find it easy to follow the stars. When our favorites are performing either on television or at an all-night sing or are moving from church to church, who has time for servanthood? Who has time to visit nursing homes? Who provides a meal for the poor? Whatever happened to the large crowd of Christians, so faithful to show up at church for the big concert, when you begin to organize calling teams?

Let us not fault the Christian artists who sing or preach for us. They are being paid for their job, and they have a duty to perform for the glory of God. They have the responsibility to help *us* praise God, too. But let us place the burden of

Christian response to human need where it really belongs: on the shoulders of the people who come to enjoy the good feelings of their old-time religion but are rarely, if ever, moved to faithful servanthood.

For consider what a huge indecency it would be to God for us to get so caught up in our own religious experiences, expressions, and feelings that we fail to see and respond to the needs of those around us. When the Christian's worship perceptions become so secularized that he languishes in the entertainment without applying the message, then those with dirty feet will remain dirty still.

Spontaneity: Letting God Move Through Our Mood

I remember him only because he shared the quietly eloquent language of tears. At times his great shoulders heaved under the weight of burden. Yet there was never a hint of attention getting, of hoarse bawling. You'd find his form draped across the altar when seekers came. His spirit was always lovely, never self-seeking. When I asked about him, Dad remarked, "He is a true Jeremiah, a weeping prophet of our day." For all I know, he wept for me, too.

Few were just like him. But I remember others who walked the aisles and shouted and praised God, who waved handkerchiefs, who lifted their hands heavenward, who laughed the innocent laugh of holy joy. I never doubted their authenticity in demonstration.

But there were many more who did not express their emotions in such outward ways. They sat quietly or wiped a tear. Their personality did not lend itself to such demonstration. Theirs was the expression of joy that came from quietness and confidence. And neither did I question their faith, however quiet.

Historically, Nazarenes were unafraid to express their emotions in public worship. The young church then was

55

formed in an era of great emotional expression. While we cannot generalize, it is safe to say that many churches today are not as emotionally expressive as they were a century ago. Perhaps people of this generation are reacting against what they felt was unnecessary emotionalism from earlier generations. Not wanting to identify themselves with what they perceived to be "whipped-up froth," they have turned to respectability. Either emotionalism or formalism is dangerous. But naturally we are interested in the best use of emotional behavior for God.

In no way can we deal with the complexities of the mind and spirit in this book. But we are interested in understanding that privilege of heartfelt religion, spontaneity. For the purpose of Christian worship, let us define spontaneity as the Spirit-led freedom to combine honestly felt conviction with sensibly expressed emotions. The result may be holy joy, tears, anxiety, and so on. The best test of sensibly expressed emotions is, after all, "not how high you jump, but how straight you walk when you hit the ground"—as I've been reminded.

It will help us also to distinguish between emotion, emotions, and emotionalism. *Emotion* is a moving or feeling inside of you, while *emotions* are the kinds of feelings expressed (such as sorrow, fear, joy, guilt, anger, etc.). *Emotionalism* is the tendency toward emotional excitement or behavior, or the likelihood of being emotional. Emotion is one of three major properties of the mind, the other two being volition (or will) and intellect.

Obviously all three—emotion, volition, and intellect —are essential for the experience and expression of worship. Sometimes emotion seems to receive more attention of the three. Thus we are often in the position of reminding ourselves to be fair with our (and others') emotional behavior.

Perhaps the reason that emotional expression is so often

eyed suspiciously or praised roundly is that we desperately need it in our services—but we need it to flow honestly and with genuine authenticity. Spontaneity simply cannot be counterfeited and worked up without a severe loss of credibility. Pastors, evangelists, musicians, and other worship leaders have a most responsible role in being sure that what comes comes naturally! Spontaneity comes when the *overflow* of the Spirit's ministry results in the *outflow* of human expression. And when that happens, move aside! For there is nothing more glorious this side of heaven than the free, uninhibited flow of the movement of God. The reliability of spontaneous emotional expression has its genius in the combination of (1) unrehearsed emotions, (2) obedience to impressions known to be from God, and (3) sensitivity to the mood of a given worship service.

It is interesting to note even as far back as the day of J. G. Morrison, that he "exhorted his followers to avoid 'boisterous praying, great bodily exercise,' and 'vociferous and constant shouting'"[15] in public services. This squares with a more contemporary observer of worship, noted church music authority Donald Hustad, who was cited by Dinwiddie:

> It is so easy to "mistake physical pleasure for spiritual blessing." That a person has been emotionally excited does not automatically mean that God has been glorified. An aesthetic "high" is not necessarily a spiritual one. One of the great powers and simultaneous dangers of music is its ability to stir the emotion directly without first having to go through a rational process.[16]

Therefore, trying to be spontaneous at the expense of genuineness distorts the intent of worship. G. T. Speer, founding father of the "Singing Speer Family," sensed this tension more than a half century ago. He encouraged his children to "feel emotions without hysteria," and this music philosophy has helped produce one of Christian music's most credible examples.

Authentic expression is the need. Wardlaw reminds us that authentic expression in worship, "rather than forcing a counterfeit emotionality, gives opportunity for the fears, joys . . . tensions and loneliness . . . to come into play. . . . Meaningful psychological expression in worship . . . not only strives for realism, but also for a healthy outflow of feeling."[17] The call is simply for balance. In an article for *Standard,* one of the presuppositions for worship listed by Fletcher Spruce is seriousness: "All frivolity and human hilarity must be set aside in order for the spirit of worship to settle down."[18] And the same author balanced this focus with the need for holy demonstration:

> Let's have a little emotion in every service—a little holy groaning and laughter, a few Amens along, maybe a tear now and then, maybe a spontaneous testimony. . . . Doing things "decently and in order" does not imply a stiff, formal, dry, cold service. Let the preacher sparkle a bit, weep occasionally. Let the laymen open up with some spontaneous demonstration and freedom "in the Spirit."[19]

Perhaps our worship definition of spontaneity seems more clear: *it is the Spirit-led freedom to combine honestly felt conviction with sensibly expressed emotions.*

Such a wonderful balance in a service, in which we have the freedom to express ourselves and the assurance that our expression has a sense of "holy order," does not come cheaply. There is a price to be paid.

First, we must be willing to avoid a judgmental, critical spirit. If somebody is expressive, so be it. If somebody else is quiet, so be it. Perhaps the genius of God's creation is its diversity. We are not all alike, and we will not all worship alike. There is room in the Kingdom for everybody. We will need to make room for ourselves and allow room for others. To become critical because some seem formal and others seem informal divides the body and misses the beauty of freedom to worship. Willingness to lay aside personally held opinions, preconceived notions, fears, and slow-to-die memories indicates maturity and flexibility.

Second, we must not confuse style with spirituality. A more formal style does not imply spiritual superiority any more than an informal style implies the blessing of God. Formality is not an excuse for deadness any more than informality is an excuse for haphazardness. Style is simply the way folks worship. Spirituality is the quality of a relationship with God. Churches where people rarely, if ever, shout may have the blessing of God as much as churches where shouting is a weekly occurrence. Public worship certainly ought to be the expression of our religion in ways that are honest and God-honoring. But the expression of our religion in worship is a freedom we lose if we moralize unjustly.

Third, we must let God define the blessings. In public worship, we must pay the price of letting God do what He wants to do. We are just there to stand back and let Him do it. Of course, that does not mean we come unprepared. We do all we can, for getting ready for the great event of worship is an ethical issue which demands our finest commitment and preparation. But after that is done, we must get out of His way. And we must respond to Him in the way that is honest for us. If He gives blessings, we humbly accept them. If it seems that a given service is "dead," we examine our hearts, refuse to judge others, and thank Him for being God.

But too often we come expecting to receive blessings which either He is not prepared to give us or we are not ready to receive. This is the trap of living in the age of "success theology." Many Christian groups advertise: "Give to God and you'll get a blessing in return! Just have a little more faith, and when you pray and praise Him, He will bless and benefit you." Such biblically untenable thinking cannot be reconciled with the sovereign nature of God. (What about those poor, loyal Christian souls who pray, ask, and truly believe, and nothing happens?) Bruce Leafblad recorded in an interview with *Leadership* magazine:

> So much of our recent history has been slanted toward developing a receiving mentality as Christians: God exists to meet our needs, to give us blessings, to fill us up. So when we come to church, it is with our hands cupped open so they can be filled again. We have become professional beggars in the courts of the Lord, and we have to turn that around so we see ourselves as "offerers," not "receivers."[20]

If we fail to note this warning, then we are tempted to judge God and our blessings from Him according to what He *does* for us in our worship—when in fact worship is something *we* do to show our love for Him!

The mood of the worshiper, then, is not dependent on what we get, how we are blessed, or even the style of the service. The mood of the worshiper is that of obedience to the impressions of the Spirit so that we sense the price God paid for us to be able to worship Him. And what price was that? The blood of His Son, Jesus. When King David visited Araunah the Jebusite to worship on his threshing floor, Araunah asked the king why he came to visit.

> "To buy the threshing-floor from you to build an altar to the Lord . . ." Araunah answered . . . "I beg your majesty to take it and sacrifice what you think fit. . . ." Araunah gave it all to the king for his own use and said to him, "May the Lord your God accept you." But the king said to Araunah, "No, I will buy it from you; I will not offer to the Lord my God whole-offerings that have cost me nothing" *(2 Sam. 24:21-24, NEB).*

Hustad comments on this passage: "For too many people, worship is simply 'getting a blessing.' . . . I think it is fair to ask the people of God—the leaders in worship as well as the whole congregation—What has it cost you to offer to God your 'sacrifice of praise'?"[21] In contrast to any selfish motive, you will note the sacrificial, servanthood model from Heb. 13:15-16, NEB: "Through Jesus, then, let us continually offer up to God the sacrifice of praise, that is, the tribute of lips which acknowledge his name, and never forget to show kindness and to share what you have with others; for such are the sacrifices which God approves."

The price of spontaneous worship? It is ever and always the movement of the Spirit through the obedient mood of the worshiper. In our humanity, we will always be tempted to glorify the unnecessary, to sit passively by and watch the performance, to miss the moving of the Spirit in our mood. So,

> The question we should be asking ourselves on the way home on Sunday morning is not, "What did I get out of it?" but rather, "How did I do?" For when all the sermons have been preached, all the anthems sung, all the worship renewal workshops conducted, and all our innovations come and gone, that is all that will have mattered: that we said with our whole being, "Worthy is the Lamb who was slain, to receive power and wealth and wisdom and might and honor and glory and blessing."[22]

4

Premise

Earning the Right to Assess Worship

"How Firm a Foundation"

As a worshiper from both pulpit and pew for many years in many places, I've observed a variety of contrasting experiences.

I've watched as ushers scrambled from all corners of the sanctuary to "take" rather than "receive" the offering. I've seen other ushers move with the stiff precision of a military drill team.

I've heard the quiet refrains of Bach from the organist's offertory, and I've tried to refrain from hearing organs at church that sounded like organs at funerals.

I've listened to the odds and ends of announcements so oddly assorted and so sadly unrelated to worship. I've heard preachers sing and singers preach. I've been in services where people seemed not to respect the house of God, and I've been in other services where coughing could be mistaken for spontaneity. I've observed pastors sing solos, pray all the prayers, make the announcements, lead the singing, and preach. And I've worshiped in services where the music and sermon followed two different tracks.

Once I visited a famous old church in Boston where worshipers sat in family pews, followed strictly a printed order of worship, and watched the minister climb pulpit stairs before preaching. Once I listened as Dr. Harold J. Ockenga, then pastor of Park Street Congregational Church in Boston, delivered a moving sermon on the ministry of the Holy Spirit. Once I was in a church when the soloist did not show up and someone offered the services of an old friend. The "old friend" heartily responded on the way to the platform, while selecting a song, "Well, there's always one thing about us: If we have an order of worship we can pitch it, for who needs a bulletin to tell you how to praise God?" Several "Amens" resounded approvingly.

In all honesty, I hasten to say that none of the above are weekly fare for most of our churches. Worship hopefully occurs regardless of how good or bad a job we make of it. Certainly God is patient to honor our worship effort, though too much of the time we do not approach the seriousness of our task with much reflection. In too many places the unnecessarily haphazard ways of our worship methods and practices often hide the significance, beauty, and grandeur of this sacred event. The good news is that God takes what we offer Him in worship and understands our spirit. The better news is that, considering who God is, every worshiper can reconsider the ways of his worship and learn to do a more adequate job.

Really? Who is to say? Who is to say that the way you and your church worships needs reconsideration or assessment? Truthfully, nobody is in place to assess worship unless he has earned the right to do so. Pastors and worship committees may offer bold suggestions or make foolishly sweeping change. But unless they have earned the right by gaining respect and the approval of people, frustration is sure to result.

Worship renewal does not occur by changes in style, tearing down traditions, or faulting things we do not like. Worship renewal comes in a climate of assessment, not an atmosphere of conflict and distrust. Change may come, but change is not the intent of reliable assessment. Assessing worship just means having a "look see" in order to determine perceptions and expectations. Our goal here is to help pastors and laity assess worship by earning the right to do so. This is the premise or foundation in answering, "Who can tell if we worship well?" Let's look at several guiding principles which will help us earn the right to assess our worship.

A. Pastoral: The Pastor's Role in Creating Worship Renewal

Worship assessment rises or falls on the interest and commitment of the pastor. If he encourages and supports it, worship assessment can be an effective ministry. If not, it does not have much of a chance.

No pastor is the sole creator of worship renewal, though he must have an active part in initiating purposeful thinking and planning. "Clergy cannot be employed to revitalize a congregation; they can only be instrumental in assisting the congregation to develop its own vitality."[1] Renewal is the result of mutual ministry between pastor and people.

Elton Trueblood, certainly a 20th-century spokesman for the lay ministry movement, states that "renewal will not come merely by the acts of professional renewers or by hierarchial operations."[2] In other words, the pastor must be a part of the process by setting himself as a role model. He must initiate times of congregational self-assessment so that laity may think critically and compassionately together.

"The task of leaders is to help create the conditions under which members will decide to activate themselves."[3] Communication is the key!

Pastors may encourage member activation simply because of their position as shepherds. Developing a spirit of trust and freedom in which laity are called to accountable reflection presupposes a pastoral style that is willing to listen and respond. Trueblood notes, "The pastor is important, not because he is wiser or better than other men, but because he is so placed that he may be able to draw out and direct the powers of other men."[4]

Of course, a strong lay ministry is at the core here. Unless professional ministers release ministry into the hands of the laity, there will be no lay ministry. Pastors must completely accept the reality that "the lay ministry . . . will not emerge in power unless it is consciously and deliberately encouraged, and it will not be encouraged unless there are able pastors and teachers to perform this liberating task."[5] Thus the pastor becomes, simply, an activator of the laity.

If pastors release some of their authority and power wisely, the end result can be a laity free to enter into mutual expressions of assessment. There is nothing automatic about pastors being so trusting or laypersons being so prepared. Pastors must see each Christian as a member of Christ's team and set about to train and equip them for service. As the pastor begins to value the potential of laity, worship assessment will come from the life of the people and not his office. Honest self-expression occurs in such an atmosphere!

So, then, a nonthreatened pastor encourages rather than smothers lay initiative. A healthy organizational climate depends upon pastors who are decisive and unafraid to create a forum for healthy lay ministry. Martin Marty underscores this:

> The more important leadership appears the more decisive pastoral leadership must be. The minister is a player-

coach, a participant-observer in lay life. . . . Laypeople do not know how to be assertive in the face of weak leaders; they need and desire the presence of someone who has a vision to try out on them, who dares to risk a statement which they can revise or refute or replace.[6]

Nothing generates trust, in my opinion, more than encouraging the laity to perform the ministries they rightfully deserve to perform.

The pastor's role in creating worship renewal becomes that of providing ample room for honest, credible feedback from the laity. For in a very real sense "too many laymen and clergy sit silently . . . hiding their feelings and ideas. . . . Time, energy, ideas and skills are wasted on a fantastic scale."[7] It may be trite, but it is true: Pastors have the privilege—and duty—of making worship assessment more than an ideal of which to dream.

B. Theological: The Ephesians Model— A Rationale for Sharing Ministry Together

It was he who gave some to be . . . pastors and teachers, to prepare God's people for works of service, so that the body of Christ may be built up until we all reach unity in the faith and in the knowledge of the Son of God and become mature, attaining to the whole measure of the fullness of Christ *(Eph. 4:11-13, NIV)*.

If any biblical concept needs to be lifted from the dusty shelves of antiquity and placed in the life of the local church, the above passage deserves the honor. To state it in all its simplicity and force, the people of God are to do the works of service for the edification of Christ's Church. Leadership roles may belong to a few, but all Christians have jobs to do. (Certainly there must be more reason than rhyme to *that* sentence.)

While pastors must encourage lay ministry, it is up to the laity to "catch" the concept of the "priesthood of all

66

believers," a phrase championed by Martin Luther. Quoting theologian-historian Philip Schaff, Oscar Feucht writes in *Everyone a Minister,* "This principle implies the right and duty of every believer to . . . take an active part in all the affairs of the church according to his peculiar gift and calling."[8]

We have greatly underestimated the power and usefulness of a laity properly trained and unleashed for service within the Body of Christ. Pastors are enablers/equippers, but they must not do the work that the saints are to do! The RSV renders Eph. 4:12, "To equip the saints for the work of ministry, for building up the body of Christ." Ray Stedman says, "Pastors, particularly, must restore to the people the ministry which was taken from them with the best of intentions."[9] The work of the ministry was never meant to suffer monopolization from professional clergymen. Indeed, such a condition gave birth to the Reformation.

Neither the apostles, prophets, pastors, teachers, nor evangelists are to do the work of the ministry, for "those tasks are to be done only by the people, the ordinary, plain vanilla Christians."[10] The church must never lose her sense of appreciation for the ministry that may be performed when its "ordinary" men are stirred to service. As Trueblood puts it, "If we take religion seriously as was done in the early Christian church . . . pastors would not be performing while others watch, but [would be] helping to stir up the ministry of the ordinary members."[11]

As pastors and laity come to value one another's gifts, the "servant" style as a model for the church will blossom. Nothing lifts the level of the laity more than a pastor who recognizes the unique role they fill. In so doing, worship becomes an avenue of ministry both to the church and the world. James Christensen agrees: "The church does not exist for its own comfortable enjoyment of worship; it is a redeemed community for ministry to the world."[12] The goal is not to see our mission as a way to find refuge and ease. The goal is to apply our mission to others. And the pastor's task is to prepare the laity for such an endeavor. Otherwise, we lose our identity as suggested by Catholic theologian Avery Dulles: "The concept of service must be carefully nuanced so as to keep alive the distinctive mission and identity of the church."[13]

Pastors have the role of liberating laity by initiating the processes and creating the climate for them to become true "ministers." But the laity, even those who visualize themselves as "ordinary," must see the theological value of the Ephesians model as a rationale for sharing ministry. Then you have an unbeatable combination.

C. Conceptual/Practical: Ownership— The Door of Approval

If the laity are involved in the thinking and planning stages of worship assessment, then their ownership of future goals or changes is naturally increased. Goal ownership occurs when people have a say, air their feelings, and have a direct part in the creation and development of decisions. As Ernest and Nancy Bormann have written in *Effective Committees and Groups in the Church,* "Members who help make and who are responsible for decisions are usually more fully committed to them and work harder to implement the action."[14]

Involving people in decisions, and thereby gaining their support and commitment, is one of the most legitimate ways to gain approval. *Not* making members a part of decision-making processes often guarantees alienation! When professionals pass goals "from the top down" upon people, ownership cannot honestly be felt. Mutual ownership spares the laity from isolation and prevents the pastor from autocratic domination. Daniel Katz and Robert Kahn, in *The So-*

cial Psychology of Organizations, support the need for sharing decisions: "People have greater feelings of commitment to decisions in which they have a part, or in which they act autonomously."[15]

The ideal and real world need not be completely separated. It is ideal and it is possible for goal fulfillment and involvement to be achieved. An involved laity tend to be a resourceful laity, a people who are capable of seeing their own goals for the church fulfilled. "The more one finds his or her personal goals fulfilled, the more intensely one becomes involved in the life of an organization."[16] This is a key factor in strong lay ministry development.

Usually, worship goals for people are unexamined and private. Services continue to be conducted, but frustration continues, too, because involvement in worship planning is something most laymen never enjoy. Unless there are functioning worship committees, such avenues just do not exist. High ownership occurs where the members and friends of a church feel that they may be heard. It is so true that "persons are much more likely to share power, to contribute their resources, when the congregation incorporates their personal goals into congregational goals and then supports and encourages persons to work to attain these goals."[17] Simply, people who attend a church must have a voice if they are to feel needed.

But an issue often overlooked is how the pastor feels about giving up his role as the worship planner and thinker. If a pastor invites suggestion, is he actually giving up his job? Does it mean that he does not know what to do? Does it imply weakness? Or does he gain respect for refusing to monopolize a given area of church life? Part of the answer lies in how the laity perceive their pastor. Most Nazarenes have assumed that of all church areas, the pastor should surely "take command" in worship. Yet, with a little encouragement and guidance, the laity will have very helpful things to say about public worship. Wardlaw's words must be heeded:

> Too many clergy today operate from nineteenth-century models of leadership that display paternalistic rugged individualism. Such a leadership sets the example, calls the shots, takes the risks, and does most of the work. . . . But such gestures of participatory decision-making cannot gloss over the fact that laity do not own the process of determining the problem, setting the goals and establishing the steps for arriving at those goals.[18]

The broader the base of those who truly own worship assessment, the greater will be the approval level when evaluation time comes. Pastors can create a climate of trust in which people are free to discuss openly their perceptions and expectations. Pastors can encourage a spirit of harmony and patience. Pastors can even release their long-standing "rule" over worship. But be fair with pastors! Perhaps no one has ever encouraged *them* to see that the best form of leadership involves a wide base of ownership.

D. Sociological: Leadership Development— Accountability in Small Groups

Just as Moses sought to "provide . . . able men . . . to be rulers" (Exod. 18:21), so we see the need for transferring power, ministry functions, and leadership responsibilities to others. This can be done by sharing information, clarifying issues, making decisions, and modeling trust. All contribute to a healthy worship climate. Training a cadre of leaders to function accountably in small groups is a most useful way of transferring trust while broadening the base of lay leadership.

The pastor needs to be an effective "weatherman," constantly gauging the climate or atmosphere of his church. The single issue of the pastor's leadership style determines the success or failure of healthy assessment. Harvard University's classic work *Motivation and Organizational Climate,* by George Litwin and Robert Stringer, has provided empirical evidence that "the manager's leadership style is a critical determinant of organizational climate."[19] For the pastor, that simply means he must be able to read the church's "weather" and at the same time value the input of lay leadership. Such a forum for testing success may be home and congregational meetings where human responses are not buried in the bulk of "paper information" so common to surveys, questionnaires, and so on. Leland Bradford and Robert Blake, coauthors of *Group Development,* stress the need for an atmosphere that is made possible by democratic leadership: "The leader may make his greatest contribution by creating an atmosphere permitting free expression of opinion and unity of purpose."[20]

The proving grounds at this point may be the careful development of lay leaders, who assume leadership of small groups set up for the purpose of assessing worship. In this way, the pastor is able to transfer to the laity his leadership style of openness to constructive criticism. The pastor's willingness to model trust and confidence in the laity is more important than being sure they agree with all of his personal opinions! We know that to be true, and hearing it from such an authority as Norman Shawchuck helps: "Good management will broaden a church's decision-making base. . . . Church members want a greater share in the decision-making. They want the structures and policies of the church to be public and open for critical examination."[21]

Developing leaders depends upon the pastor-manager's ability to delegate power and decision-making opportunities to the laity. The result will be a more healthy organizational climate due to high levels of trust and confidence. Good signals are given: "You have important gifts to offer"; "Your word is as needed as my word"; and

"This issue is something you must own as yours, not one you take because you like me."

There is a sense in which the laity are in touch with the church in a way that the pastor is not. They feel the pulse of their peers. Without question the pastor must "know the score" and be sensitive to his people. But the church members will make comments and offer suggestion to trusted friends whom they see as responsible leaders. Trained leaders will be able to gather the interests of the people because they are engaged in a group process that values mutual trust. "Management involves both organizational and spiritual leadership, and it requires that leaders work through and with people to achieve the group's goals and purposes."[22]

Wise is the pastor, then, who is willing to transfer his own trust and confidence to respected lay leaders so that they, in turn, will invest personal time and energy in goals they care about. Trueblood's comment is so apropos: "Though it seems strange that it should be so, it is a fact that one man, rightly placed in the ministry, can make an enormous difference in the lives of other men and in the total impact of the Church on the world."[23] The pastor must be that "rightly placed" man. He must be capable of transferring his understanding of ministry to key lay leaders so that they, in turn, model genuine ministry before the entire parish.

E. Biblical: God as Worthy of Our Worship

Earning the right to assess worship means seeing clearly that God is worthy of our best effort. God's worthiness is affirmed biblically, but it is not always expressed adequately in our worship of Him. This may be true because in our humanity we cannot comprehend fully God's divine nature. We seem to have difficulty grasping His greatness and majesty in a way that honors *Him*. We know *who* God is, but we

72

are prone to forget that He is *God.* If we ever comprehend fully that God must be *God,* it might change considerably much of what we do in worship. Worship is to enable us to focus upon the very holiness of God. Many times our scattered thoughts lead us a thousand ways during worship. And we have a way of justifying many of them. Greathouse reminds us,

> We evangelicals rejoice in our "Body Life," as we should; but our worship tends in some churches to be too much a reflection of *our* experience in Christ. Great hymns like "Holy, Holy, Holy" and "O God, Our Help in Ages Past" lose their depth of meaning in man-centered worship; then our services tend to become exercises in showmanship and decibels. The celebration of our oneness in Christ is precious, but it must not be divorced from the sense of God's sublime glory and matchless grace which move true worshipers to be "lost in wonder, love, and praise."[24]

Earning the right to assess worship means knowing that if God *is* worthy, then we must find ways to instill a sense of awe within the worshiper so that he is willing to examine his *own* perceptions faithfully. We must come to the point that we ask ourselves, "Why *are* we in church on Sunday, and what will we do about our response to God on the day set aside for His glory?" Adam Clarke offers, "Worship . . . implies that proper conception we should have of God, as the great governor of heaven and earth, of angels and men."[25] For this to occur, a biblical view of God's greatness must be seen.

First Chron. 16:29 provides a helpful view: "Give unto the Lord the glory due unto his name: bring an offering, and come before him; worship the Lord in the beauty of holiness." From this, worship is seen as *our* responsibility: We praise Him for who He is. Yet many of our services of worship have stressed doing things for God and getting blessings for ourselves rather than expressing truthful praise.

If we see ourselves as the worshipers and God as the One who is to be worshiped, it helps us keep perspective.

The Psalmist encouraged this: "Know ye that the Lord he is God: it is he that hath made us, and not we ourselves; we are his people, and the sheep of his pasture" (Ps. 100:3). Here God is described "as the Creator and Sustainer of our existence."[26] We cannot help but see the majesty of God! For "when we worship we do not worship an equal; we worship our creator, the eternal, infinite God. . . . In worship man experiences a creature-feeling, a feeling of dependence upon God."[27]

Such a biblical view of God's worthiness is set in stark contrast to an indifferent, casual worship attitude that pervades much of evangelicalism today and is noted by John R. W. Stott, rector emeritus of All Souls Church in London.

In an article titled "Transcendence: Now a Secular Quest," published in *Christianity Today,* Stott bemoans the way in which the evangelical church has lost its sense of transcendence, its sense of connection with "the fear of the Lord." He feels the church, with all its potential in Christian worship, has nearly bequeathed its rite of meditation to the world, and that meditation is now "a secular quest." Stott's concern is that our craze for "close encounters" and preoccupation with extraterrestrial mysteries of the universe

> constitutes a powerful challenge to the quality of our Christian public worship. Does [our worship] offer people what they are seeking . . . so that we bow down before the Infinite God in that mixture of awe, wonder and joy which we call "worship"?
>
> "Not often." . . . We evangelicals do not know much about worship. Evangelism is our specialty, not worship. We have little sense of the greatness of Almighty God. We tend to be cocky, flippant, and proud. And our worship services are often ill-prepared, slovenly, mechanical, perfunctory and dull. . . . Much of our public worship is ritual without reality, form without power, religion without God.[28]

What can the church do about such an indictment? Most certainly we cannot hide from it. Rather, we must commit ourselves to the biblical view of knowing that God deserves so much more than He is getting from us. Of course, in our frailty we will *never* give God all the glory He deserves, but we can give Him our best! And our best means knowing that God paid a great price for *us* to be able to sing, "Worthy is the Lamb that was slain" (Rev. 5:12).

F. Historical: The Need for a
Worship Perspective Among Nazarenes

Enabling a people to tap their own historical worship roots as individuals and as an entire church (or denomination) is another way of entry into worship assessment. This will not be easy, if only because each of us sees his past in terms of his own understanding. It is not easy to confess to needed change in the ways of our worship, too. After all, praising God cannot usually be judged in terms of "right" or "wrong." But we can look at worship both subjectively and objectively.

Perhaps for most of us, surfacing our own perceptions of worship and listening as others do so has its trials. For the truth is, most of us feel we are right. And for *personal* perceptions and memories, we may be. But as each blends his own history, or perception of it, with others, we see through quite a variety of lenses. Frustration comes in trying to strike a sense of unity about both our history and present worship activity. The sad result is that many of us sense the impending fruitlessness of such assessment and give up. Then at that point, our own perception of our historical roots becomes even more neglected—and firmly embedded in our minds. By default, then, we allow a false sense of sophistication to obscure the thing we should be most clear about—our heritage. As Neil Wiseman teaches us,

> Often in the past, my lack of understanding of the worship roots of our Protestant heritage gave me a kind of silly

pride. I reasoned, my spiritual roots are in the free, spontaneous kind of services, so I do not need to know about the forms, history or theology of worship. . . . [However] I must know more about the wide variety of worship understanding in the history of the church if I am to have an accurate basis for really appreciating my own religious heritage. . . . The conclusion of the matter lingers with me still—worship deserves more attention from all of us simply because it is at the heart of the church's work.[29]

His words depict my reluctance to probe an area of church life that seemed to limp steadily along regardless of what was done or not done to it. I could not have been more wrong. Remaining blind to need does not erase the need. It only encourages blindness. And blindness, in turn, breeds insensitivity to one's worship needs as well as those needs of others.

Wardlaw speaks clearly about the results of insecurity and fear on the part of those who develop a loss of worship identity. Remaining in touch with our history while seeing the need of the day in which we live may spare us from the lopsidedness of which Wardlaw speaks:

> A significant part of our emotional investment in liturgy is wrapped up in the fixity and immutability embedded in the experience. We long for one hour in the week when at least some of the ground beneath our feet is not shifting sand. "Good old" hymns, sermons in the language of Canaan, prayers that soar on the sounds of more innocent years, sung responses fixed in our bones, become ingredients so many of us depend on for . . . stability in a runaway world.[30]

Surely no sensitive worshiper wants to treat his heritage with callous contempt. If we err at all, it is perhaps in the other direction, which is that of so "camping out" in our heritage that we fear *any* difference in worship style, custom, or tradition. Thus we fear necessary change or assessment because we associate it with the loss of a very dear memory or even a trend toward "modernizing" current worship.

But an honest assessment of our heritage will help us *honor our past* while at the same time appraise current need. Honesty should bear the fruit of patience with our fellow worshiper's views so that reflection is done in a spirit of sensitivity. We must remember that honoring our heritage means much more than making mental note of historical data. For me to assess my worship with integrity, I must see my religious faith in light of my father's and grandfather's religious faith. Worship assessment is never done in a historical vacuum. Our generation cannot be cut off from the whole of Christian history and be seen in its true perspective. Worley has wisely said,

> Many of our difficulties today are due to our inability to be responsible history-making people in our time. We do not seem to be able to look at our history from the perspective of present faith commitments and see the inappropriateness for us of much of that created by men in previous generations.[31]

To earn the right to assess today's worship, a people must know their personal and corporate history. Appreciating the diversity of each worshiper within your church is so crucial. Michael Novak's *Rise of the Unmeltable Ethnics* speaks of the need people have to value their cultural and national heritage within the larger framework of society. But this needs to be done within the "melting pot" of a local congregation, where people gather with such contrasting opinions and varied experiences. Says Novak, "What I should like to do is to come to a better and more profound knowledge of who I am, whence my community came, and whither my son and daughter, and their children, might wish to head in the future: I want to have a history."[32] Well put. And the worshiper needs just such a spirit.

It is time for us to say how much we appreciate our personal and corporate worship heritage. Uncovering long-hidden perceptions—and misperceptions—is a privilege that makes clear the mission of today's worship practice. And it shows we have not forgotten our root system. As Carl Dudley writes, "By honoring our history we can satisfy our need to say thanks to the past."[33]

The whole of worship is an act of remembrance. Earning the right to assess worship can be done in no finer way than to value deeply the worship heritage that has brought us to this hour.

5

Participation

Involving the Laity
in Worship Assessment

"To Serve the Present Age"

Once pastor and people agree that congregational worship needs to be assessed, the inevitable question arises: "How is it done?" Perhaps the question could be better stated: "How can we assess faithfully our worship in a way that assures both credibility and a degree of accuracy?"

This chapter will include some examples of exercises that address that question. But it is fruitless to begin with "how to" methods unless both pastor and people commit themselves to honest "theologizing" about the nature of assessment itself. Theologizing is an oversized word, perhaps, but it simply means trying to deal with an issue—such as worship—in a way that is faithful and accountable to a biblical revelation of God.

For our purposes this suggests the assessment of our perceptions of God, church music, sermons, or other worship activities that have theological meaning. We then make comparisons with fellow worshipers in a spirit of compassionate candor. It means that we examine our memories, our future dreams, our understanding of the meaning of persons as these relate to worship activity. Theologizing does not mean *teaching* a theology of worship so much as it does trying to discover and define our worship theology in a way that is faithful to the Bible, respectful of our own traditions, and conscious of the contemporary world in which we worship.

This requires honesty about our local church's worship. Faithfulness in defining how and by what means or activities we will assess worship is needed. Honesty must be the motivating issue if people are heard and if their feelings are accepted. Too often it is easier not to ask questions because we fear differences of opinion, new suggestions, and frustration. But the church is never assessed in silence. So theological integrity demands that the people of God be perceptive, reflective, patient, and truthful regarding worship assessment. Usually we have an abundance of rhetoric, "but theological reflection on the ways in which love, power, and justice should prevail in the organizational life of the church is almost totally lacking."[1]

We cannot leave theologizing to chance. Involving laity in worship activities that let them examine issues deep within the fabric of human experience is vital. This lifts the worth of laity by not merely asking opinion but calling for them to engage in *self-* assessment. Further, involving the laity proves that assessment is *their* responsibility since they are the church. Theological integrity is placed in jeopardy if pastors do all the assessment, planning, and ministering. For honesty to bear its full weight upon the church, the laity must have the privilege of personal reflection. That's good "theologizing"!

Here's a way to illustrate the focus of our assessment. When you see the interdependency that is needed in fair assessment, it will help. Imagine that you draw three circles, representing: (1) the Church of the Nazarene within the whole of Christian worship history; (2) your own personal worship memories and understanding; and (3) the current worship you now experience as it is placed in the contemporary world. Looking at the diagram below, observe the middle area where each of the circles overlap. This shaded section is the focus of interdependency. That's where true assessment occurs. Worship cannot be seen realistically by looking only at yourself, your own feelings, or your current worship interests. It must be seen in light of the world you are trying to reach, your heritage, and the worship interests of others in your church. Getting into the "intersection" where these circles overlap spares those who assess from being lopsided.

Turn, now, to several types of tools or activities which may be useful in evaluating worship. None of them are foolproof and without human error. They are not designed for serious academic research, but they should provide a variety of lenses through which to see congregational worship.

A. A Teacher's Outline for Classes on Christian Worship

The following is an adaptation of an outline suitable for teacher use.[2] This class enables the student to assess worship by comparing sights and sounds of worship in which the teacher may present both tape recordings and 35-mm slides that depict worship activity.

CLASS 1—ASSESSING MY PERCEPTIONS OF WORSHIP

1. Setting My Sights: Learning Objectives for This Class

   A. Enabling participants to grasp individual perceptions of the nature of Christian worship.

   B. Assisting students in determining personal attitudes toward worship.

   C. Helping participants to become aware of worship likes and dislikes.

   D. Trying to define and determine "acceptable worship."

   E. Comparing individual and group responses.

2. Setting My Plan: Learning Exercises for This Class

   A. *Exercise 1:* Presentation of 25 "sights and sounds" of worship. (See fig. 2.) This will be used with the 30-second tape-recorded sounds (organ, singers, etc.) and the 30-second viewing of 35-mm color slides. Concurrent with this will be the student's use of the "Assessment of Worship Perceptions Check Sheet" (fig. 1), and with the "Personal Attitude Check Sheet" (fig. 2). (Note: Figures 1-8 are found at the end of this chapter, page 91.)

   B. *Exercise 2:* Discussion of the student's "Assessment of Worship Perceptions Check Sheet." A time to raise worship perceptions and ideas, and encourage similarities, differences, and so on. (20 min.)

   C. *Exercise 3:* Presentation of "Personal Attitude Check Sheet" in which students notice the words they circled that contributed to their reactions and feelings. (20 min.)

   D. *Exercise 4:* Discussion of "Personal Attitude Check Sheet" in which students may compare worship perceptions with others.

E. *Exercise 5:* Final analysis, learnings, class evaluations. (Complete survey in fig. 3.) Each exercise should be approximately 20 minutes in length.

3. Setting the Scene: Study and Materials for This Class

   A. *Preparatory study materials:* Development of 25 audiovisual aids and check sheets for discussion of worship assessments and attitudes; development of questionnaire to assess worship perceptions.

   B. *Other materials needed:* Cassette recorder with taped "sounds" of worship (quartet, sermons, etc.); 35-mm slides showing "sights" of worship; projector, screen, pencils, and so on.

4. Step-by-step: Through the Learning Exercises

   A. *Exercise 1: Presentation of 25 "Sights and Sounds."* Following an explanation of class learning objectives, I will present the "Assessment of Worship Perceptions Check Sheet." When the direction of the check sheet is clarified, I will present each of the "sights and sounds" on both cassette or screen, giving time for students to note responses. This exercise is designed to elicit individual perceptions regarding the nature of worship.

   B. *Exercise 2: Discussion of the "Assessment of Worship Perceptions Check Sheet."* Students will be encouraged to note differences by comparing their perceptions with others. Discovering personal perceptions will be the issue. This will enable members to determine if they are similar or different from the group. It will have the advantage of valuing individual worship perceptions.

   C. *Exercise 3: Presentation of "Personal Attitude Check Sheet."* In this exercise I will rerun the "sights and sounds" so that students may be able to check exactly why they hold the perceptions they do. This checklist will provide specific word-association rationale.

D. *Exercise 4: Discussion of "Personal Attitude Check Sheet."* This "second look" at our initial responses will help the student see his reason for his perceptions. Giving students opportunity to do this publicly helps them to explain their feelings.

E. *Exercise 5: Final Learnings, Class Evaluations.* In this section we will explore particular personal learnings which are of interest for the group. I will encourage students to enter their learnings in a Worship Class portfolio which will be provided at this first class.

5. Looking Ahead: The Next Unit

At this time, the teacher may explain the topic and direction of the next class. It will help the student to have some understanding of the content of the whole course. The public gathering of the mix and flow of worship perceptions is a healthy way of addressing a neglected area of congregational life.

6. Final Survey: Evaluating Our Learnings

The following questionnaire provides a way to measure student response, as well as gauging teacher effectiveness for this class (see fig. 3).

Note: Other such classes would need to be developed on these topics: worship and acquaintance with God; the significance of music and preaching in worship; the value of the sacraments; worship as enablement for witness to the secular world; determining a theology of worship; gathering our unique heritage and worship "roots."

B. The Use of Home and Congregational Meetings

I would strongly encourage the use of an agenda for training home meeting leaders and secretaries, and you may note figure 4 as an example. Home (as well as congregational) meetings are attempts to meet in both the small-group and corporate context so that assessment may be done. The advantage of home meetings is their informal nature, plus the fact that key lay leaders have been trained to listen to their own peers. You will note the directness and simplicity of this approach. By the time strong laypersons have agreed to assist, be trained, and lead home meetings, the bulk of the work is done. The rest is a matter of being sure leaders see the value in group participation in order to gather the attitudes and heartfelt expressions of the church body.

The particular direction of home meetings will be noted in figure 5. You will see in the "Time Line for Home Meetings" (fig. 5) that several major areas of worship assessment are encouraged. I have provided more than sufficient questions which are designed to encourage not only discussion of worship but appraisal of our individual perceptions of worship.

After the home meetings have been held, it is vital to meet that night with the leaders and secretaries (in some cases a husband-wife team) over coffee to debrief, gather responses, and so on. The material needs to pass from "paper shuffling" to the careful interpretation of major issues to help the worship committee or appropriate group.

Congregational meetings have the advantage of being in the church building where the whole body may address given issues. As with all public meetings, plenty of announcements and interest remove the element of secrecy. It is just an opportunity for the church to see the entire fellowship in pursuit of a common goal. That in itself is a healthy process. Figure 6 is a proposed design for gathering congregational expectations. Pastors may divide the church into small groups either before or after the congregational meeting. As with all home or church-wide meetings, a sense of connection with current need is necessary. Figure 7 is provided in an attempt to facilitate individual commitments.

C. Discovering a Nazarene Worship Profile

The following is an adaptation of a statistical tool used to gather worship memories among a group of Nazarenes in the central United States in 1979.[3] It attempts to collect the *earliest* worship memories of Nazarenes and may be used in a local church to compare "old-timers" with newer people.

Please Circle Only One Number for Each Item

	Always	Usually	Sometimes	Rarely	Never
THE PURPOSE OF WORSHIP					
1. The purpose of worship was seeing souls saved.	1	2	3	4	5
2. Our worship emphasized praising God.	1	2	3	4	5
3. Our worship emphasized evangelism.	1	2	3	4	5
4. Our worship emphasized liturgy.	1	2	3	4	5
5. I remember worship as being informal.	1	2	3	4	5
THEOLOGICAL FAITHFULNESS IN WORSHIP					
6. Preaching was expositional.	1	2	3	4	5
7. Preaching was topical, based on a theme.	1	2	3	4	5
8. Preaching told of God's love and forgiveness.	1	2	3	4	5
9. Preaching told of God's wrath and judgment.	1	2	3	4	5
10. We understood the "dos and don'ts."	1	2	3	4	5
11. Communion was held regularly.	1	2	3	4	5
12. We used to practice baptism in worship.	1	2	3	4	5
13. Preaching about sanctification was clear.	1	2	3	4	5
14. We understood what tithing meant.	1	2	3	4	5
15. The altar was used a lot in our worship services.	1	2	3	4	5
HISTORICAL FAITHFULNESS IN WORSHIP					
16. The Apostles' Creed was read frequently.	1	2	3	4	5
17. Our *Manual* was well explained during worship.	1	2	3	4	5

18. Our Wesleyan heritage was clear to us from worship. 1 2 3 4 5
19. Wesleyan hymns were sung often. 1 2 3 4 5
20. Liturgy carried a sense of formality. 1 2 3 4 5

PASTORAL FAITHFULNESS IN WORSHIP

A. About Our Worship Leaders:

21. The pastor acted alone in leading worship. 1 2 3 4 5
22. The laity helped plan our worship. 1 2 3 4 5
23. There was usually no strict order of worship. 1 2 3 4 5
24. There was much informality in our worship. 1 2 3 4 5
25. There was room for freedom in the Spirit. 1 2 3 4 5
26. Nazarenes were clock-conscious. 1 2 3 4 5

B. About the People of God:

27. People took part in our services of worship. 1 2 3 4 5
28. People were accepted "warts and all." 1 2 3 4 5
29. People gave money because needs were great. 1 2 3 4 5
30. Singing was enthusiastic and informal. 1 2 3 4 5
31. People "got blessed" during our worship. 1 2 3 4 5
32. People were stylish in their dress. 1 2 3 4 5
33. Many poor visited our services. 1 2 3 4 5
34. People often prayed out loud together in worship. 1 2 3 4 5

C. About Our Place in Worship

35. People usually sat in the same place each week. 1 2 3 4 5
36. The sanctuary was a place of great sacredness. 1 2 3 4 5
37. The little children attended with the adults. 1 2 3 4 5
38. Our sacred feelings inhibited us. 1 2 3 4 5
39. Our worship style created a sense of formalism. 1 2 3 4 5
40. Our altar was freely used; not a decorative piece. 1 2 3 4 5

MISSION FAITHFULNESS IN WORSHIP

41. We took offerings for the poor during worship. 1 2 3 4 5
42. We were sacrificial for world mission offerings. 1 2 3 4 5
43. We welcomed the poor as well as the rich in worship. 1 2 3 4 5
44. Worship services were evangelistic. 1 2 3 4 5
45. Many unsaved attended our services. 1 2 3 4 5

D. Measuring Differences Between Worshiping Christians

This survey was used to separate differences in the way people perceived their worship habits. The terms "affectionate" and "directional" are borrowed from Carl Dudley of McCormick Theological Seminary.[4] The learning will come in seeing that "affectionate Christians" are usually more people oriented, whereas "directional Christians" are generally more task or goal oriented. Worshipers will be gauging themselves in three areas: their sense of *place* (physical location) in worship, their sense of *people,* and their sense of *presence* (of the holy or "numinous") in worship. Responses to the extreme left indicate affectionate attitudes; responses to the extreme right indicate directional attitudes.

PLACE: Why was a particular *place* important to you?

1. The altar was where I received spiritual help and felt close to God.

1. The altar was where I learned biblical truth.

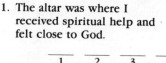

2. We used the altar mostly for prayer and confession.

2. We used the altar mostly for rituals such as Communion.

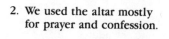

3. I enjoyed sitting with friends and visiting at church.

3. I liked to sit alone where I could see or hear the best.

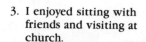

4. The sanctuary was a place of spontaneity and joy where we enjoyed fellowship in the Lord.

4. The sanctuary was a place of hush where the order of worship dictated seriousness.

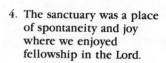

PEOPLE: What do you remember about *people* in worship?

1. There was much singing, testifying, and "noisy freedom" among us.

1. Nazarene were quiet, dignified, and tended to be reserved.

$$\overline{1} \quad \overline{2} \quad \overline{3} \quad \overline{4} \quad \overline{5} \quad \overline{6} \quad \overline{7}$$

2. Nazarenes started church when they were ready and didn't worry too much about the clock.

2. Nazarenes were very clock-conscious and always began and ended right on time.

$$\overline{1} \quad \overline{2} \quad \overline{3} \quad \overline{4} \quad \overline{5} \quad \overline{6} \quad \overline{7}$$

3. Nazarenes worshiped in a spirit of fellowship and just wanted the Lord to lead.

3. Nazarenes were more interested in worshiping "decently and in order" than anything else.

$$\overline{1} \quad \overline{2} \quad \overline{3} \quad \overline{4} \quad \overline{5} \quad \overline{6} \quad \overline{7}$$

4. Nazarenes gave time, talent, and tithes because they felt they belonged to the church and its fellowship.

4. Nazarenes gave time, talent, and tithes because they had a sense of stewardship and duty.

$$\overline{1} \quad \overline{2} \quad \overline{3} \quad \overline{4} \quad \overline{5} \quad \overline{6} \quad \overline{7}$$

PRESENCE: How do you remember the *presence of God* in worship?

1. God is remembered because of *what He did* among us: healings, answered prayer, and so on.

1. God is remembered because of *what He was* in the universe: Creator, Sovereign God, and so on.

$$\overline{1} \quad \overline{2} \quad \overline{3} \quad \overline{4} \quad \overline{5} \quad \overline{6} \quad \overline{7}$$

2. A spirit of reverence existed because God seemed to be in our midst.

2. A spirit of reverence existed because God seemed to be "in His heaven."

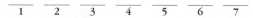

| 1 | 2 | 3 | 4 | 5 | 6 | 7 |

3. We pleased God because we expressed our feelings freely in worship.

3. We pleased God because our services were well organized.

| 1 | 2 | 3 | 4 | 5 | 6 | 7 |

4. Communion was a time when we felt comforted and touched by the Holy Spirit.

4. Communion was a time when we pondered anew our responsibility and mission to the world.

| 1 | 2 | 3 | 4 | 5 | 6 | 7 |

When this tool is used, it would be interesting to note differences in age-groups, since this will show generational differences in the perception of congregational worship. As with most surveys, anonymity is essential. However, people may not mind giving their age. Being able to rank the results by "teen," "young adult," "middle adult," and "older adult" shows the similarity and disparity that exist. Having worshipers to state their ethnic identity (such as Black, Hispanic, Polish, Greek, etc.) provides yet another lens to see their perceptions. While it will not be true in every case, most individuals tend toward "affectionate" or "directional" personality types. This has significant bearing upon the way worship is remembered and perceived.

Figure 8 is a sample of the kind of questionnaire which provides closure and final analysis. For Worship Committees and those who plan worship, knowing the pulse of the church is so important. Questionnaires and surveys merely give information on paper, though it is crucial. If properly designed these methods can be specific, attainable, and measurable. But needed most is person-to-person care.

ASSESSMENT OF WORSHIP PERCEPTIONS CHECK SHEET

Item		Very Positive	Little Positive	Middle	Little Negative	Very Negative
	1					
You are to respond	2					
to all sights and	3					
sounds as if you are	4					
experiencing them in	5					
the context of public	6					
worship in the	7					
sanctuary.	8					
	9					
Please respond	10					
according to your	11					
first emotional	12					
reaction rather than	13					
according to what	14					
you think you	15					
"ought" to feel.	16					
	17					
A "middle" response	18					
can mean either you	19					
are torn between	20					
two extremes or you	21					
do not have a strong	22					
feeling one way or	23					
the other.	24					
	25					

Fig. 1

"What Influenced Me Most?"

PERSONAL ATTITUDE CHECK SHEET

Circle the word(s) contributing most to your reactions. This will provide a rationale for your perceptions. Look for meaningful repetition of your responses in the vertical columns.

ITEM	CONTENT	PEOPLE	VOICE	OBJECTS	INSTRUMENTS	BUILDING
1. PIX: spire	beauty					spire
2. "God's Kids"		children	voices		instruments	
3. PIX: choir in church		choir		cross		interior of church
4. PIX: glass stained	color	Christ		glass		
5. Johnny Hall			voice		drums, piano	
6. PIX: General Assem.	church gathered	large crowd				
7. Singing Policemen	beauty	male duet	voices		organ	
8. PIX: cemetery				grave markers		mausoleum
9. PIX: church	location			cross		architecture
10. Messiah	style	solo	voice		organ	
11. G. Braun	style		voice		percussion	
12. PIX: SS children	SS scene	children teacher		alabaster box		
13. PIX: Gr. Holy Temp.	feeling			cross		architecture
14. Mozart	recital				piano	
15. PIX: formal church				tower		spire
16. Moody Choir	Luther's hymn	choir	voices		organ	
17. Peter Marshall	diction	sermon	voice			
18. Merrill Womack	feeling	singer	voice		piano and strings	
19. PIX: offering plate	giving			money and tithe box		
20. Blues' duet		vocal duet	voices		guitar	
21. PIX: windows	color			stained glass		interior
22. PIX: orchestra		action			orchestra	interior
23. Millhuff	sermon	preacher				
24. PIX: Grand Tetons	majesty			mountains		
25. Rex Nelson Singers		singers	voices		percussion, guitars	

These represent the "sights and sounds" (the pictures and taped recordings) which were useful in gathering people's perceptions of worship memories. Various recordings of singers and preachers, plus photos of "worship-type" symbols serve to make clear attitudes and perceptions of worship.

Fig. 2

WORSHIP CLASS SURVEY RESULTS
Evaluation of Class 1

1. Looking at the sights and sounds helped draw out my perceptions of worship.

   Agree ___ ___ ___ ___ ___ ___ ___ Disagree
         1   2   3   4   5   6   7

2. I discovered that most of my perceptions of worship were similar to those of our group.

   Agree ___ ___ ___ ___ ___ ___ ___ Disagree
         1   2   3   4   5   6   7

3. I do not have very many strong feelings about worship.

   Agree ___ ___ ___ ___ ___ ___ ___ Disagree
         1   2   3   4   5   6   7

4. I believe worship planning and thinking should be done by the pastor and not the laypeople.

   Agree ___ ___ ___ ___ ___ ___ ___ Disagree
         1   2   3   4   5   6   7

5. There are many things about worship that are not really clear to me.

   Agree ___ ___ ___ ___ ___ ___ ___ Disagree
         1   2   3   4   5   6   7

6. I can worship better alone than with the people of God in church.

   Agree ___ ___ ___ ___ ___ ___ ___ Disagree
         1   2   3   4   5   6   7

7. What I saw and heard in this class affected me as much as how I felt.

   Agree ___ ___ ___ ___ ___ ___ ___ Disagree
         1   2   3   4   5   6   7

8. After this class, I am more inclined to think that worship involves things I had not seriously considered before now.

   Agree ___ ___ ___ ___ ___ ___ ___ Disagree
         1   2   3   4   5   6   7

Fig. 3

AGENDA FOR TRAINING HOME MEETING
LEADERS/RECORDERS

1. PURPOSE: To train laypeople in the skill of eliciting congregational feedback in assessing worship perceptions and expectations.

2. NATURE: Use of small-group home meetings to create an atmosphere of togetherness, trust, and informality.

3. YOUR TASK:
   A. As Leader: to serve as a small-group leader by facilitating group discussion; gaining feedback in a responsible manner.
   B. As Recorder: to record all information; collect evaluations.
   C. Your Reward: seeing people involved in caring about the direction of our church; modeling trust to gain trust; releasing authority to gain the respect of others.

4. MY TASK:
   A. To offer training, instruction, guidance, material, strategy.
   B. To offer my support, faith, and trust in you as a leader/recorder.
   C. To offer participative leadership as we share mutual ministries.
   D. To allow you to stand on your own strengths/skills, and your commitment to the renewal of our worship activities.

5. OUR TASK:
   A. To build group cohesiveness through our stated purpose.
   B. To build interdependence through teamwork.
   C. To build unity through the creation of a wholesome "work climate."
   D. To secure congregational trust in *us* as leaders by gaining *their* (the people's) input; to refuse to feel threatened by different ideas.
   E. To gain congregational ownership by showing *our* faith in the purpose.

6. THE REASON FOR YOUR SELECTION: The special interest, skills, knowledge, and leadership strengths you possess related to worship is testimony to your commitment and concern.

7. ITEMS WHICH HELP SMALL GROUPS TO FUNCTION EFFECTIVELY:

A. Openness expressed from leader; informality void of communicating unpreparedness. Special time at beginning to secure first names of people.

B. Identifying early in the meeting why you are together: to gather congregational feelings and attitudes about worship perceptions and expectations.

C. Be sure recorder is ready to list significant information, both positive and negative.

D. Remember: You are not trying to obtain group agreement, but to seek input.

E. Keep the group on the subject!

F. Communicate that this is not a "gripe session" to simply unload criticism. For every complaint, ask people to give a positive solution or reasonable way out of the problem.

G. Seek to make your group a time for idea gathering, information distributing, and support gaining.

H. Ask questions to less participative people; be willing to suggest that this task is one the whole group should work on, not just a few dominant voices.

I. Refuse the temptation to talk too much yourself!

J. Assure people that what they offer is worthy, that it counts, and that the worship committee and church board are prepared to receive their information and direct the congregation along the most reasonable path. (This builds integrity into what you are doing.)

K. Since you are a realistic person, be sure suggestions seem reasonable. If you feel like a comment seems unrealistic or hard to live with, ask, "How could we carry that out?" or, "Would you be willing to serve with a committee that was expected to carry out this suggestion?"

L. Avoid getting bogged down in trivia! This is a simple design and lends itself to free discussion.

M. Express gratitude for the group's responsiveness.

Fig. 4

TIME LINE FOR HOME MEETINGS

7:00-7:10—Getting started and acquainted; coffee served.

7:10-7:30—Encounter 1: Assessing New/Reinforced Learning from the Worship Classes
  1. Is our current worship true to Christian history? How are we different from the Early Church of the New Testament? From early Nazarenes?
  2. What definite changes have you seen in our worship practices in your lifetime?
  3. Are you clear about the purpose of our worship? Do we understand the kind of God we are worshiping?
  4. Other questions:

7:30-7:45—Encounter 2: Assessing Our Activities of Worship
  1. List the activities we do that either help or hinder effective worship. Be sure to give solutions.
  2. How do you know God is given adequate praise in our worship activities?
  3. Does the Holy Spirit have sufficient freedom to move unhindered in our worship? If not, what do you suggest?
  4. Would you recommend any changes?
  5. Other questions:

7:45-8:15—Encounter 3: Assessing Our Responsibilities
  1. How can we improve our relationships to one another because of our worship?
  2. Does our worship enable us to show caring concern for those in our local church family? How? How not?
  3. What difference should our worship on Sunday make in our world on Monday? How do you feel about financial self-denial or sacrifice in offerings as a way of making worship connect with life and the needs of others aside from our local needs (such as Thanksgiving and Easter offerings)?
  4. How does our worship enable us to tell a poor man that God loves him? If we come to give praise to God what does that mean in terms of showing caring concern to our community?
  5. Is our worship responsibly fitted to our age and to our society? What sense of burden for the lost (unsaved) is put upon us because of our worship?

96

8:15-8:45—Encounter 4: Assessing Our Expectations for More Meaningful Worship Experiences in the Future

1. What way-of-life changes in our worship are important? Why do you feel this way?
2. Do the people or the pastors own worship? Whose task is it? Why do the pastors usually do all the planning for worship?
3. How would you suggest that laypersons have more input and feedback into the conducting and evaluation of worship? How could we encourage laypeople to take a more responsible role in planning worship services and activities?
4. What personal commitments would be demanded through worship activity if we lived out some of our expectations? Please be specific.
5. What separation should be made between worship and entertainment?

8:45-8:50—Evaluation of Our Meeting
Simply distribute the questionnaire, have your group make their notations, and collect. No names signed, please.

(Note: Not all surveys and questionnaires that might be helpful are included. Pastors or worship leaders could design surveys to fit their own congregation.)

Fig. 5

CONGREGATIONAL MEETING DESIGN
(CONGREGATIONAL EXPECTATIONS)

1. EXPECTATIONS ABOUT ASSESSMENT AND CHANGE:

Does our assessment indicate that we need changes in worship activity? Have we identified the areas needing change? What expectations do you have about any desired change in our worship activities?

2. EXPECTATIONS ABOUT DIRECT INVOLVEMENT OF LAITY IN WORSHIP PLANNING:

What expectations do we have about giving laypersons opportunities for involvement in thinking and planning related to our worship? How would you like to see our people taking a more active role in this church? What would you personally like to do?

What expectations do we have about people conducting various parts of the service (such as reading scripture, making the announcements, introducing guests, leading a service, initiating a children's time in worship)? If the role of the laypersons has been passive in the past, what can be done?

3. EXPECTATIONS ABOUT END RESULTS:

What end results or outcomes should become a part of our way of life because of all this energy spent in worship planning? Or, what should church life look like a year from now because of our work? (Should we expect to see an involved laity, services that are better coordinated, more freedom in the Spirit, planning groups that meet regularly? What *do* we have a right to expect?) If worship renewal took place, how would you recognize it?

(Note: These meetings could be held on a Sunday night after church, or another time. Perhaps they could be done over a series of evenings. For most benefit, it is valuable to meet as an entire group *after* small groups have met in order to assess the interests of all. In that way, you have the exchange of ideas betwen all members so that the group hears everybody's views.)

Fig. 6

CONGREGATIONAL MEETING DESIGN
(CONGREGATIONAL COMMITMENTS)

Recognizing both the interest we have generated in congregational worship and the needs and expectations we have discussed, I would be willing to commit myself to the following areas of revitalization and ministry:

_____ serving as a member of our Worship Committee

_____ reading scripture during the service

_____ making announcements or introducing guests during the service

_____ helping to lead a service if I had some training, direction

_____ helping to create ways for children to be involved in worship

_____ singing special songs or singing in the choir

_____ being involved in the ministry of lay preaching

_____ serving on an usher team

_____ being part of a "listening team" to help *evaluate* worship services, following adequate preparation and training

_____ being part of a "liturgy team" to help *plan* worship services, following adequate preparation and training

_____ helping to teach a class on "Christian Worship"

_____ working with a drama group

_____ creating colorful banners and cloth decorations to highlight seasons of the church year, such as Lent, Easter, Pentecost, Christmas

_____ working as a support person with those who teach membership classes and discuss baptism, child dedication, and so on, with new families

_____ other:

Signed _____

Fig. 7

99

HOW WELL DID WE ACHIEVE OUR GOALS?

1. How good of a job did we do in giving laypeople opportunities to share opinions about church life?

2. How helpful were the worship classes? How well did they help you identify and share perceptions (understanding) of Christian worship?

3. The home meetings were spent in evaluating our current worship practices. Why was this a success or failure for you?

4. The congregational meetings were spent in evaluating our personal worship expectations and commitments. How was this helpful?

5. How have you grown as a layperson by being involved in this worship assessment process?

6. What have you learned about yourself? Do you see any changes in your perceptions? Do you see worship about like everyone else?

7. What would you like to see continued as a way of periodic public evaluation for our people?

_____ further teaching in a worship class.
WHY:

_____ continue with home meetings.
WHY:

_____ continue with congregational meetings.
WHY:

8. What would you personally like to see changed, if possible, in our worship? Is this a personal feeling or a group need?

9. How are you more sensitive to the worship needs of other people because of this congregational self-study?

10. How is our church more committed to worship renewal, having gone through this assessment process?

Fig. 8

100

6

Praise

Refining the Art

"Praise Ye the Lord, the Almighty"

The fine art of Christian public praise is an art worth improving! Considering all God has done for us, how could we ever thank Him and praise Him enough? Moreover, considering *who* God is, our praise for Him must know no limit. The following are several pastoral suggestions relating to the art of praise and worship of God. Certainly this is not a full list, nor may each of these apply to each reader, depending upon varying levels of spiritual and emotional maturity. Nonetheless, refining the art of praise is the Christian's priority in worship.

First, the art of praising God is an act of devotion, and if there is no devotion to begin with then there is no praise. Simply, praise cannot be given to God if sin rules the heart, for if God is to be praised He must first be loved.

Sin is the great preventer of praise. Sin is a blockade, a barrier to the possibility of praise. People may come to church, give offerings, sing the hymns of the faith, and follow the motions of worship; but if sin is in their hearts they cannot truly praise God because they do not even love Him enough to serve Him.

I do not doubt God's ability to hear the sinner's prayer, nor the sinner's ability to pray. But it can be seriously questioned whether or not a person has the capacity to worship God, let alone appreciate His will, if he lives in broken fellowship away from God. The Psalmist's words "If I regard iniquity in my heart, the Lord will not hear me" (66:18) indicate God's attitude toward one hiding sin in his heart. Obviously, this does not mean that God is indifferent or uncaring. But it does mean that if sin remains covered up, God will not annul His justice merely to answer prayer. How can there be fellowship with God if sin remains unconfessed? How can praise be received as sincere if the heart and life are disobedient?

Sin as a way of life presents a moral breach between the sinner and God so that praise is subverted. Honest praise comes from an honest heart. One who walks in rebellion has no love for God. Thus to assume that a sinner will praise God genuinely and faithfully is to assume that giving honor is possible without giving love.

But how would God like that? Perhaps no more and certainly less than a parent would like it if a child showed respect for his father but refused to give an ounce of loving-kindness. It would be a strained and unreal relationship indeed. The only legitimate way to show honor and worth to God *is* to love Him! Otherwise praise is perfunctory, shallow, empty. Genuine praise demands an obedient and honest heart.

Note that it is possible to go through the motions of praise, but that worship does not occur merely because motions are correct. Going through the motions is a sad commentary on the life of one who tries by sheer dint of human effort to praise God from a heart that is full of sin.

This is why people who are awash in sin find worship

services so disturbing or convicting. Sin darkens the lens through which the majesty of God is seen. Therefore, the first step is not to refine the art of praise but to purify the heart of the praise-giver.

Second, refining the art of praise does not mean praising the art of refinement. One of the many confusing myths that always surface when discussion about worship renewal begins, is that renewal means "trying to get dignified." We must simply not give in to such illusion. Refining worship means making it better, just as you might refine a song, a sermon, or a witness. Since you are giving your praise to the King of Kings, it only seems logical that you'd want to do your best. If the president of the United States called you and said he'd be at your home for a dinner, just with you and your family, you'd be sure to have the house clean, the best dishes out, and you'd want your children not to chew with their mouths open. Why? Only because something important was to happen. Obviously, doing our best in the performance of worship is not wrong! It does not imply that we are sophisticated when we refuse to give God any old thing in worship just because He is patient.

If we *did* praise the art of refining our customs, our ways, our traditions more than God, then our value system would need to be evaluated. After all, reverence and stylishness must not be confused.

Most importantly, trying to do our best for God in the refinement of worship does not mean that we lose the blessing of God! While God can assure us with a sense of His blessing regardless of whether we do everything just right, that is not a license for us to move haphazardly or aimlessly through our praise of Him! The fact that we love Him enough to rehearse songs, construct expositional sermons, and wear our Sunday-go-to-meeting clothes does not suggest that we are proud and superior. It tells God how much we think of Him *if* it is done in a spirit of reverence and humility. Further, the fact that we go to some effort to refine the art of praise does not mean that we are beyond need of His outpoured showers of blessing. Other things being equal, it would seem that God would be *pleased* to bless people who are committed to giving their very best to Him! In fact, the entirety of Psalm 150, the grand finale to the book of praise, is one tremendous ovation to the spirit of giving one's *all*— in many different ways—to the praise of God.

Third, giving God the praise He deserves means that you must be ready for the task. Refining the art of public Christian worship means that the worshiper, not merely the worship leader, has a task to perform. Public worship is a body life event. You cannot let yourself be carried along by the others and be a credible worshiper. You owe God *your* best, regardless of the quality of another's worship.

This means that preparation for worship has theological significance. Getting ready early enough on Saturday to arrive on time on Sunday, coming in a *spirit* of praise that springs from a *life* of praise and devotion, and coming with the willingness to pour out your *energy* in praise are all issues that demand something of you. You dare not come unprepared to spill yourself in the work of praise. You simply owe God a tithe of your emotions, your tears, your joy, and your intellectual commitment. To save something of yourself for God on Sunday is a volitional act that Satan will labor long and hard to subvert. Praise takes something out of you.

Let me illustrate. In my opinion, there has never been a day in which the emotional and intellectual drain upon the Christian *for seemingly legitimate reasons* has been as apparent as it is today. The vast popular appeal of Christianity is alarming if for no other reason than its rootage in the fertile minds of people who claim to give God the glory but pay no price to do so.

The price many Christians are paying to give praise to

God is too cheap. Sunday by Sunday pastors in American pulpits are preaching to people who are just too exhausted, emotionally spent, and at the point of burnout because they have involved themselves in the erosion of emotion all week long. As if the average church did not demand enough emotional energy (not to mention professional, social, and family demands), the extrachurch religious world may demand even more.

Without question this is a day unprecedented in its offer of true spiritual and emotional self-help. Numerous very worthy radio and television programs exist to aid the growth and maturity of the Christian. But much else exists, too. Christians are subjected to massive campaigns, broadcasting features, bulk mailouts, and personal solicitation by phone. They are asked to give emotional attention and financial commitment. And whether or not a given Christian ever gives a dime of his money, who can measure the tears that are shed, the anguish that is felt, and the praise so easily given in a week's time of bombardment of songs, sermons, stories, and emotional binge?

For after a Christian has watched two or three television programs so professionally done on Sunday's circuit, has involved himself emotionally in several worship/preaching events, what does he have left for his church of less than 100 attenders, a choir that practiced briefly, and a pastor not quite as good as the one on television? Probably not much at all, for the human spirit has just so much to give.

It seems that the Christian worshiper has a responsibility to be selective. He must insist that everything in a given week prepare him for the great event on Sunday morning, including the use of time, the way he spends his money, and perhaps most importantly, the expenditure of his priceless emotional energy. If praise is to be worthy, the sacrifice will be costly. And the greatest sacrifice may be in what is *not* given indiscriminately but is reserved only for the honor of God.

I, for one, do not fault the Christians who find little or no true worship in their local church and therefore turn to media sources out of a sense of desperation and spiritual hunger. Let's face it: In many places the church is *not* offering adequate fare for the worshiper who desires to truly honor the Lordship of God's Son.

But the worshiper is compelled all the more to convert his own local church into a center of honest praise, rather than allow his energies to be drained and his loyalties divided a dozen ways. I would certainly argue for the worshiper's right to dialogue with his pastor and responsible fellow worshipers until a forum was developed for worship assessment. Otherwise the worshiper is subjecting himself to constantly comparing a struggling local church situation with professionally done media presentations. But that's just the beginning. The tragic issue is that the worshiper who refuses to involve his energy in worship renewal and assessment and who refuses to prepare himself for worship in his own church home, faces the likelihood that his praise to God is divorced from personal commitment to the demands of *being* a credible worshiper. In such a way, time, talent, and tithes are lost on a fantastic scale. And in such a way, praise itself becomes suspect because it is only a token expression of our love.

We dare not be just a people of hilarious praise and yet have a hollow commitment to the worship needs of the local body of Christ.

Fourth, refining the art of praise means appreciation for "throne room" ethics. Without succumbing to the temptation to list certain rules and standards for conduct in the King's throne room—the sanctuary of the church—it is far more important that the reader and his church fellowship develop their own worship norms, or what they consider legitimate behavior in worship. Obviously, this begins in the home, not in the church, though the church ought to be the physical symbol of reverence for the community of faith.

Like you, I've seen the extremes. I have been in churches where children were allowed to wander in and out during services, where teens were not the only ones who chewed gum, and where adults have actually slept! On the other hand, I've seen such stilted formalism that the atmosphere was cold and uncomfortable.

The thing that makes for balance is a guiding principle, a worship philosophy that supersedes lists of dos and don'ts. On more than one occasion I have seen parents actually slap little children in the face because they broke the rule, forgot a family code, and so on. Rather, what is so desperately needed is such an appreciation for the greatness of the event that conduct is dictated by the value we place on worship itself.

If worship leaders and worshipers do not value or evaluate what they are doing, why should anyone else? If nobody really cares, then who will have appreciation? And if no appreciation, then it may not matter what you wear, how you behave, or what you do with an hour's worth of time. For at the heart of this is the fact that you cannot separate how people feel about worship from the price people are willing to pay to experience worship.

When we come into the sanctuary of God, everybody wants a good service. Everybody wants to go home feeling as if he has been to church. But what price will we pay? What does the quality of our service, our singing, our preaching tell our youth? What does *our* personal commitment, our time spent, our money invested, our energy given—what does all of it suggest to the next generation? It might be questioned what we ought to demand in terms of proper behavior at church for others if we ourselves give little conscious thought to the songs we sing, the sermons we preach, and the way we honor God.

Not only do I want my children to respect the house of God when they gather in the "throne room" to worship Him, but I want to be sure that I offer them a reason for praising God—a reason that is clearly evident in *my* utter amazement at being in the presence of the Almighty.

Fifth, the refinement of praise means that I must determine the source of my joy. Joy is the basis of praise. If I do not have true joy in my heart, then it will be difficult to praise adequately. Joy is not so much a feeling such as enthusiasm or excitement, as it is a state of mind such as contentment or peace. Feelings come and feelings go, and they are very important to our emotional well-being. But praising God must not be dependent upon how we feel. It is, however, essential that our praise to God be established upon true joy and not upon moment-by-moment feelings. I must be able to praise God, for example, even when I don't feel like it.

And that is why joy must come from a source that is sane, legitimate, biblical. Our "joy in the Lord" as Christians suggests the Source: God. For the Christian to find his joy, his true inner joy, in another source is to circumvent the will of God. So it seems helpful for the worshiper to see God not only as the Focus of his praise but the Source of his joy. Thus God is described as our "all in all" (see Col. 3:11).

If God is not the Source of my joy then my praise life will lose its luster. A number of years ago while on vacation with my wife and children at the ocean, I gathered up several handful of very tiny seashells. They sparkled in the early morning sun in a variety of hues: purple, yellow, white, blue, green, and violet. I lifted them from their exposure to pounding surf, scorching sun—all the elements of nature. I brought them home, cleaned them, and placed them on my library shelves along with other ocean rarities.

But in a few weeks these little rainbow-colored shells grew dim. Their colors faded, and they all began to look alike. The problem was that they were no longer in their natural habitat. They no longer drew warmth from the sunshine and moisture from the sea. And they lost their luster, their beauty, their notable distinction. They became brittle remnants of their former state. In time, I threw them away.

The Christian who draws his joy from a source other than God becomes like that. He may find pleasure and excitement. He may feel great! But without the joy of the Lord as his strength, he will eventually lose his capacity to praise. He will soon lose his beauty, his notable distinctiveness. He will be unable to show his true color. And the very things that once seemed to provide for every felt need will leave him brittle and dry.

Praise is such a fragile element. It must be handled with great care. It must not be pumped up with the thoughtless insensitivity often found in the secular arenas of life. It must not be left in the print of aged hymns of the faith. It must not be removed from its natural habitat and displayed as a showcase for the world to know that we are religious.

Praise must come from the life of joy. The life of joy must come from God. And the best way to show it is to live it from Monday through Saturday so that when we express it on Sunday there will be no doubt about its authenticity.

Otherwise, who *can* tell if we worship well?

Notes

Chapter 1

1. Neil B. Wiseman, "A Little Old Lady's Question" (editorial), the *Preacher's Magazine* 55, no. 3 (March, April, May, 1980): 1.

2. C. Peter Wagner, *Your Church Can Grow* (Glendale, Calif.: Gospel Literature International, 1976), 99.

3. Paul Waitman Hoon, *The Integrity of Worship* (Nashville: Abingdon Press, 1971), 30.

4. Robert C. Worley, *Dry Bones Breathe!* (Chicago: Center for the Study of Church Organizational Behavior, McCormick Theological Seminary, 1978), 11.

5. Hans Küng, *Truthfulness: The Future of the Church* (New York: Sheed and Ward, 1968), 162.

Chapter 2

1. Franklin M. Segler, *Christian Worship: Its Theology and Practice* (Nashville: Broadman Press, 1967), 26.

2. Ilion T. Jones, *A Historical Approach to Evangelical Worship* (Nashville: Abingdon Press, 1954), 13.

3. Ibid., 20.

4. Ibid., 21.

5. Ibid., 19.

6. Ibid., 30.

7. Ibid., 31.

8. Ibid., 33.

9. William H. Willimon, *Word, Water, Wine, and Bread* (Valley Forge, Pa.: Judson Press, 1980), 15.

10. J. D. Douglas, ed., *The New International Dictionary of the Christian Church:* "Early Church Worship," by Ralph P. Martin (Grand Rapids: Zondervan Publishing House, 1974), 1062.

11. Segler, 24.

12. Ibid., 25.

13. Jones, 74.

14. Ralph P. Martin, *Worship in the Early Church* (Grand Rapids: Wm. B. Eerdmans Publishing Co., 1976), 33.

15. Ibid., 80.

16. Segler, 28.

17. Ibid., 29.

18. James F. White, *Introduction to Christian Worship* (Nashville: Abingdon Press, 1980), 26.

19. Jones, 85.

20. Arthur S. Hoyt, *Public Worship for Non-Liturgical Churches* (New York: Hodder and Stoughton, 1911), 37.

21. Ibid., 39.

22. George W. Fiske, *The Recovery of Worship* (New York: Macmillan Co., 1931), 128.

23. Jones, 124.

24. S. F. Winward, *The Reformation of Worship* (London: Carey Kingsgate Press, 1964), 104.

25. Nathaniel Micklem, ed., *Christian Worship* (London: Oxford University Press, 1936), 137.

26. Jones, 124.

27. Kenneth G. Phifer, *A Protestant Case for Liturgical Renewal* (Philadelpha: Westminster Press, 1955), 70.

28. Jones, 254.

29. Fiske, 128.

30. Ibid.

31. Harry Emerson Fosdick, *Great Voices of the Reformation* (New York: Random House, 1952), 497.

32. Horton Davies, *Worship and Theology in England,* 3 vols. (Princeton, N.J.: Princeton University Press, 1961-65), 3:195.

33. Raymond Abba, *Principles of Christian Worship* (London: Oxford University Press, 1957), 132.

34. Davies, 3:196.

35. Ibid., 201.

36. Jones, 257.

37. Trevor Dearing, *Wesleyan and Tractarian Worship* (London: Epworth Press, 1966), 44.

38. Evelyn Underhill, *Worship* (New York: Harper and Brothers, Publishers, 1937), 305.

39. John Bishop, *Methodist Worship in Relation to Free Church Worship* (London: Epworth Press, 1950), 108.

40. Ibid., 71.

41. Ibid., 151.

42. Phifer, 98.

43. Ibid., 100.

44. Donald W. Dayton, *Discovering an Evangelical Heritage* (New York: Harper and Row, Publishers, 1976), 16.

45. Ibid., 102.

46. Charles E. Jones, *Perfectionist Persuasion: The Holiness Movement and American Methodism, 1867-1936* (Metuchen, N.J.: Scarecrow Press, 1974), 82.

47. F. Ernest Stoeffler, ed., *Continental Pietism and Early American Christianity* (Grand Rapids: Wm. B. Eerdmans Publishing Co., 1976), 210.

48. Mendell Taylor, *Handbook of Historical Documents of the Church of the Nazarene* (Kansas City: Mendell Taylor, Publisher, n.d.), 4.

49. Ibid., 38.

50. B. F. Haynes, ed., *Herald of Holiness* 1, no. 1 (April 17, 1912): 13.

51. Haynes (April 24, 1912), 1:13.

52. Haynes (June 12, 1912), 1:13.

53. Haynes (August 14, 1912), 1:4.

54. J. B. Chapman, ed., *Herald of Holiness* 34 (September 24, 1945): 13.

55. Chapman (November 16, 1945), 34:13.

56. F. A. Hillery, ed., *The Beulah Christian* (Providence, R.I.: Pentecostal Printing Co., February 22, 1908), 17:n.p.

57. C. B. Jernigan, *Pioneer Days of the Holiness Movement in the Southwest* (Kansas City: Pentecostal Nazarene Publishing House, 1919), 42.

58. *Proceedings of the First Annual General Assembly* (Los Angeles: Nazarene Publishing Co., 1907), 11.

59. *Proceedings of the Second Annual General Assembly* (Los Angeles: Nazarene Publishing Co., 1908), 29.

60. *Proceedings of the Fourth Annual General Assembly* (Kansas City: Pentecostal Nazarene Publishing House, 1915), 19 ff.

61. Taylor, 219.

62. Ibid.

Chapter 3

1. W. T. Purkiser, *Called unto Holiness: The Story of the Nazarenes, The Second Twenty-five Years: 1933-1958* (Kansas City: Nazarene Publishing House, 1983), 56.

2. Gene Van Note, *The People Called Nazarenes: Who We Are and What We Believe* (Kansas City: Nazarene Publishing House, 1983), 101.

3. Don M. Wardlaw, "Tension in the Sanctuary" (McCormick Theological Seminary, n.d.), 6.

4. William M. Greathouse, "Worship as Recognition of the Holy," *The Preacher's Magazine* 55, no. 3 (March, April, May, 1980): 5.

5. Ibid., 4.

6. Ibid.

7. Purkiser, 66, 69.

8. Jon Johnston, *Will Evangelicalism Survive Its Own Popularity?* (Grand Rapids: Zondervan Publishing House, 1980), 15.

9. Ibid., 26.

10. Ibid., 25.

11. Timothy L. Smith, *Called unto Holiness: The Story of the Nazarenes, The Formative Years* (Kansas City: Nazarene Publishing House, 1962), 315.

12. Wardlaw, 3.

13. Greathouse, 5.

14. Richard D. Dinwiddie, "Moneychangers in the Church: Making the Sounds of Music," *Christianity Today* (June 26, 1981): 18.

15. Smith, 316.

16. Dinwiddie, 18.

17. Don M. Wardlaw, "Letting the Whole Person Worship" (Chicago: paper at McCormick Theological Seminary, n.d.), 1.

18. Fletcher Spruce, "Presuppositions of Worship," *Standard* 35, no. 24 (June 14, 1970): 1.

19. Spruce, "Overcome the Ho-hum in Worship," *Standard* (October 29, 1967), 5.

20. Muck, Terry C., ed., "Worship: Preparing Yourself and Your Congregation," *Leadership* 2, no. 3 (Summer 1981): 114.

21. Donald Hustad, "Music and the Worship of God," *The Preacher's Magazine* 55, no. 3 (March, April, May, 1980): 52.

22. Ben Patterson, "Worship as Performance," *Leadership* 2, no. 3 (Summer 1981): 52.

Chapter 4

1. Worley, 10.

2. Elton Trueblood, *The Incendiary Fellowship* (New York: Harper and Row, Publishers, 1967), 114.

3. Worley, 69.

4. Trueblood, 36.

5. Ibid., 37.

6. Martin E. Marty, "If I Were to Build Again," *The Christian Ministry* (November 1978), 7.

7. Robert C. Worley, *Change in the Church: A Source of Hope* (Philadelphia: Westminster Press, 1976), 103.

8. Oscar E. Feucht, *Everyone a Minister* (New York: Family Library, Pyramid Publications, 1974), 34.

9. Ray C. Stedman, *Body Life* (Glendale, Calif.: Regal Books, 1972), 79.

10. Ibid., 81.

11. Elton Trueblood, *Your Other Vocation* (New York: Harper and Row, Publishers, 1952), 52.

12. James L. Christensen, *Don't Waste Your Time in Worship* (Old Tappan, N.J.: Fleming H. Revell Co., 1978), 124-25.

13. Avery Dulles, *Models of the Church* (Garden City, N.Y.: Doubleday and Co., 1974), 95.

14. Ernest G. Bormann and Nancy C. Bormann, *Effective Committees and Groups in the Church* (Minneapolis: Augsburg Publishing House, 1973), 80.

15. Daniel Katz and Robert Kahn, *The Social Psychology of Organizations* (New York: John Wiley and Sons, 1966), n.p.

16. Robert C. Worley, *A Gathering of Strangers: Understanding the Life of Your Church* (Philadelphia: Westminster Press, 1976), 30.

17. Ibid., 31.

18. Wardlaw, "Tension in the Sanctuary," 3.

19. George H. Litwin and Robert A. Stringer, Jr., *Motivation and Organizational Climate* (Cambridge: Division of Research, Graduate School of Business Administration, Harvard University Press, 1968), 169.

20. Leland P. Bradford, ed., *Group Development* (La Jolla, Calif.: University Associates, 1974), 72.

21. Norman Shawchuck, "Church Management: The Architecture of Ministry," *Christianity Today* (July 20, 1979), 19-20.

22. Ibid., 19.

23. Trueblood, *The Incendiary Fellowship,* 35.

24. Greathouse, 4.

25. Adam Clarke, *Christian Theology* (Salem, Ohio: Convention Book Store, H. E. Schmul, 1967), 226.

26. Greathouse, 5.

27. Segler, 59.

28. John R. W. Stott, "Transcendence: Now a Secular Quest," *Christianity Today* (March 23, 1979), 37.

29. Neil B. Wiseman, "Worship—More than a Spectator Sport," *The Preacher's Magazine* 55, no. 3 (March, April, May, 1980): 8.

30. Wardlaw, "Tension in the Sanctuary," 6.

31. Worley, *Change in the Church: A Source of Hope,* 47.

32. Michael Novak, *The Rise of the Unmeltable Ethnics* (New York: Macmillan Publishing Co., 1975), 83.

33. Carl S. Dudley, *Making the Small Church Effective* (Nashville: Abingdon Press, 1978), 101.

Chapter 5

1. Worley, *Change in the Church: A Source of Hope,* 30.

2. The "sights and sounds" concept was borrowed by permission from Don M. Wardlaw, professor of preaching and worship at McCormick Theological Seminary, Chicago, and adapted for use in a class taught by the writer. The six major division titles for Class 1 are also borrowed from Dr. Wardlaw.

3. The "Nazarene Worship Profile" was mailed to 300 ministers and laypersons on the Central Educational Zone of the Church of the Nazarene. There were 155 responses returned. This was part of the research completed by the writer for studies at McCormick Seminary.

4. The "affectionate"/"directional" concept was borrowed by permission from Dr. Carl Dudley of McCormick Seminary, and adapted to fit the survey used to assess worship in a local congregation.

Bibliography

Abba, Raymond, *Principles of Christian Worship*. London: Oxford University Press, 1957.

Bishop, John. *Methodist Worship in Relation to Free Church Worship*. London: Epworth Press, 1950.

Bormann, Ernest G., and Nancy C. Bormann. *Effective Committees and Groups in the Church*. Minneapolis: Augsburg Publishing House, 1973.

Bradford, Leland P., ed. *Group Development*. La Jolla, Calif.: University Associates, 1974.

Christensen, James L. *Don't Waste Your Time in Worship*. Old Tappan, N.J.: Fleming H. Revell Co., 1978.

Clarke, Adam. *Christian Theology*. Salem, Ohio: Convention Book Store, H. E. Schmul, 1967.

Davies, Horton. *Worship and Theology in England*. 3 vols. Princeton, N.J.: Princeton University Press, 1961-65.

Dayton, Donald W. *Discovering an Evangelical Heritage*. New York: Harper and Row, Publishers, 1976.

Dearing, Trevor. *Wesleyan and Tractarian Worship*. London: Epworth Press, 1966.

Douglas, J. D., ed. *The New International Dictionary of the Christian Church*. Grand Rapids: Zondervan Publishing House, 1974.

Dudley, Carl S. *Making the Small Church Effective*. Nashville: Abingdon Press, 1978.

Dulles, Avery. *Models of the Church*. Garden City, N.Y.: Doubleday and Co., 1974.

Feucht, Oscar E. *Everyone a Minister*. New York: Family Library, Pyramid Publications, 1974.

Fiske, George W. *The Recovery of Worship*. New York: Macmillan Co., 1931.

Fosdick, Harry Emerson. *Great Voices of the Reformation*. New York: Random House, 1952.

Hoon, Paul Waitman. *The Integrity of Worship*. Nashville: Abingdon Press, 1971.

Hoyt, Arthur S. *Public Worship for Non-Liturgical Churches*. New York: Hodder and Stoughton, 1911.

Jernigan, C. B. *Pioneer Days of the Holiness Movement in the Southwest.* Kansas City: Pentecostal Nazarene Publishing House, 1919.

Johnston, Jon. *Will Evangelicalism Survive Its Own Popularity?* Grand Rapids: Zondervan Publishing House, 1980.

Jones, Charles E. *Perfectionist Persuasion: The Holiness Movement and American Methodism, 1867-1936.* Metuchen, N.J.: Scarecrow Press, 1974.

Jones, Ilion T. *A Historical Approach to Evangelical Worship.* Nashville: Abingdon Press, 1954.

Katz, Daniel, and Robert Kahn. *The Social Psychology of Organizations.* New York: John Wiley and Sons, 1966.

Küng, Hans. *Truthfulness: The Future of the Church.* New York: Sheed and Ward, 1968.

Litwin, George H., and Robert A. Stringer, Jr. *Motivation and Organizational Climate.* Cambridge: Harvard University Press, 1968.

Martin, Ralph P. *Worship in the Early Church.* Grand Rapids: Wm. B. Eerdmans Publishing Co., 1976.

Micklem, Nathaniel, ed. *Christian Worship.* London: Oxford University Press, 1936.

Novak, Michael. *The Rise of the Unmeltable Ethnics.* New York: Macmillan Publishing Co., 1975.

Phifer, Kenneth G. *A Protestant Case for Liturgical Renewal.* Philadelphia: Westminster Press, 1955.

Purkiser, W. T. *Called unto Holiness: The Story of the Nazarenes, The Second Twenty-five Years: 1933-1958.* Kansas City: Nazarene Publishing House, 1983.

Segler, Franklin M. *Christian Worship: Its Theology and Practice.* Nashville: Broadman Press, 1967.

Smith, Timothy L. *Called unto Holiness: The Story of the Nazarenes, The Formative Years.* Kansas City: Nazarene Publishing House, 1962.

Stedman, Ray C. *Body Life.* Glendale, Calif.: Regal Books, 1972.

Stoeffler, F. Ernest, ed. *Continental Pietism and Early American Christianity.* Grand Rapids: Wm. B. Eerdmans Publishing Co., 1976.

Taylor, Mendell. *Handbook of Historical Documents of the Church of the Nazarene.* Kansas City: Mendell Taylor, Publisher, n.d.

Trueblood, Elton. *The Incendiary Fellowship.* New York: Harper and Row, Publishers, 1967.

————. *Your Other Vocation*. New York: Harper and Row, Publishers, 1952.

Underhill, Evelyn. *Worship*. New York: Harper and Brothers, Publishers, 1937.

Van Note, Gene. *The People Called Nazarenes: Who We Are and What We Believe*. Kansas City: Nazarene Publishing House, 1983.

Wagner, C. Peter. *Your Church Can Grow*. Glendale, Calif.: Gospel Literature International, 1976.

White, James F. *Introduction to Christian Worship*. Nashville: Abingdon Press, 1980.

Willimon, William H. *Word, Water, Wine, and Bread*. Valley Forge, Pa.: Judson Press, 1980.

Winward, S. F. *The Reformation of Worship*. London: Carey Kingsgate Press, 1964.

Worley, Robert C. *A Gathering of Strangers: Understanding the Life of Your Church*. Philadelphia: Westminster Press, 1976.

————. *Change in the Church: A Source of Hope*. Philadelphia: Westminster Press, 1976.

————. *Dry Bones Breathe!* Chicago: Center for the Study of Church Organizational Behavior, McCormick Theological Seminary, 1978.

Published Articles

Chapman, J. B., ed. *Herald of Holiness,* September 24, 1945, 13.

————., ed. *Herald of Holiness,* November 16, 1945, 13.

Dinwiddie, Richard D. "Moneychangers in the Church: Making the Sounds of Music." *Christianity Today,* June 26, 1981, 18.

Greathouse, William M. "Worship as the Recognition of the Holy." *The Preacher's Magazine,* March, April, May, 1980, 3.

Haynes, B. F., ed. *Herald of Holiness,* April 17, 1912, 13.

————., ed. *Herald of Holiness,* April 24, 1912, 13.

————., ed. *Herald of Holiness,* June 12, 1912, 13.

————., ed. *Herald of Holiness,* August 14, 1912, 4.

Hillery, F. A., ed. *The Beulah Christian,* February 22, 1908, n.p.

Hustad, Donald. "Music and the Worship of God." *The Preacher's Magazine,* March, April, May, 1980, 52.

Marty, Martin E. "If I Were to Build Again." *The Christian Ministry,* November 1978, 5-9.

Muck, Terry C., ed. "Worship: Preparing Yourself and Your Congregation." *Leadership,* Summer 1981, 114.

Patterson, Ben. "Worship as Performance." *Leadership,* Summer 1981, 52.

Proceedings of the First Annual General Assembly. Los Angeles: Nazarene Publishing Co., 1907, 11.

Proceedings of the Second Annual General Assembly. Los Angeles: Nazarene Publishing Co., 1908, 29.

Proceedings of the Fourth Annual General Assembly. Kansas City: Pentecostal Nazarene Publishing House, 1915, 19 ff.

Shawchuck, Norman. "Church Management: The Architecture of Ministry." *Christianity Today,* July 20, 1979, 19-22.

Spruce, Fletcher. "Overcome the Ho-hum in Worship." *Standard,* October 29, 1967, 5.

———. "Presuppositions of Worship." *Standard,* June 14, 1970, 1.

Stott, John R. W. "Transcendence: Now a Secular Quest." *Christianity Today,* March 23, 1979, 37.

Wiseman, Neil B. "A Little Old Lady's Question." The *Preacher's Magazine* 55, no. 3 (March, April, May, 1980): 1.

———. "Worship—More than a Spectator Sport." The *Preacher's Magazine,* March, April, May, 1980, 8.

Unpublished Articles

Wardlaw, Donald M. "Letting the Whole Person Worship." McCormick Theological Seminary, n.d., 1.

———. "Tension in the Sanctuary." McCormick Theological Seminary, n.d., 3, 6.